Ultimate Flutter Handbook

Learn Cross-Platform App Development with Visually Stunning UIs and Real-World Projects

Lahiru Rajeendra Mahagamage

Orangeava.com

First published: October 2023

Published by: Orange Education Pvt Ltd, AVA™

Address: 9, Daryaganj, Delhi, 110002

ISBN: 978-93-88590-86-0

www.orangeava.com

Dedicated to

My beloved Parents

Athula Mahagamage

and

Nilanthi Karunathilake

About the Author

Meet **Lahiru Rajeendra Mahagamage**, a luminary in the world of software development and the guiding force behind your journey through the captivating realm of Flutter in his latest masterpiece, Ultimate Flutter Handbook. Armed with a Bachelor of Science degree in Information Technology, Lahiru embarked on an extraordinary career, leaving an indelible mark on the tech landscape.

With over four years of hands-on experience as a software virtuoso, Lahiru's expertise shines brightly. His journey led him to the vibrant city of Melbourne, Australia, where he currently thrives as a Flutter developer, pushing the boundaries of innovation.

Beyond his impressive academic and professional achievements, Lahiru is an educator at heart. He has passionately cultivated a flourishing YouTube channel dedicated to unraveling the intricacies of Flutter. This platform isn't just a medium for knowledge sharing; it's a community, where developers, enthusiasts, and aspiring learners converge to explore Flutter's boundless potential.

Lahiru's profound love for Flutter is a driving force behind his work. His YouTube channel is a testament to his unwavering commitment to empowering others with the skills needed to excel in this dynamic framework.

Ultimate Flutter Handbook is a manifestation of Lahiru's journey, experiences, and profound insights. In this book, he distills his wealth of knowledge into a comprehensive guide, replete with practical examples and hands-on guidance. Whether you're a seasoned developer striving to reach new heights or a curious newcomer eager to embark on a journey of discovery, Lahiru is your dedicated companion.

Thank you for choosing this book and embarking on an exhilarating learning adventure with Lahiru Mahagamage. Together, we'll unlock the full potential of Flutter and craft exceptional applications that leave an indelible mark on the digital landscape.

Acknowledgement

I would like to express my deepest gratitude to my parents for their unwavering support, encouragement, and belief in me throughout this incredible journey of writing my first book, "Ultimate Flutter Handbook." Your love and motivation have been my guiding light, and I couldn't have accomplished this without you.

I also extend my sincere appreciation to the entire team at OrangeAva Publishing Company for believing in the vision of this book and providing invaluable guidance and resources to bring it to life. Your dedication to excellence and commitment to helping authors achieve their goals are truly commendable.

To all my friends and colleagues who offered their insights, feedback, and encouragement, I am profoundly grateful. Your contributions have enriched the content of this book and made it more valuable to readers.

Lastly, to the vibrant Flutter community and all the aspiring developers eager to master this powerful framework, I wrote this book with you in mind. Your passion for innovation and dedication to learning inspire me every day. May this book empower you to create exceptional Flutter applications and embark on your own journey of becoming a pro.

Thank you all for being a part of this remarkable chapter in my life.

Preface

Welcome to "Ultimate Flutter Handbook." I'm delighted to have you as a reader on this exciting journey through the vast landscape of Flutter, Google's powerful and versatile UI toolkit for building natively compiled applications for mobile, web, and desktop from a single codebase.

Flutter has taken the development world by storm, and for good reason. Its ability to create beautiful, performant, and expressive user interfaces across multiple platforms has revolutionized the way we build apps. Whether you're a seasoned developer looking to expand your skill set or a newcomer eager to dive into the world of app development, this book is designed to be your trusted companion.

As you turn the pages of this book, you'll embark on a comprehensive and hands-on exploration of Flutter. We'll start with the basics and gradually delve into more advanced concepts. Whether you're interested in creating mobile apps for Android and iOS, developing for the web, or even exploring desktop applications, you'll find the knowledge and tools you need here.

This book is divided into nine simple chapters. Here's what you can expect from this book:

Chapter 1 will give you an introduction on what Flutter is, the benefits of using Flutter, and what types of apps can be created using Flutter and its architecture.

Chapter 2 will guide you through the installation of Flutter and running it. It will give you step-by-step instructions on requirements needed for Flutter to run, making the environment ready for development (downloading, installing and configuring of flutter SDK and IDEs), creating, running and adding assets to your first Flutter application, and understanding its folder structure.

Chapter 3 will focus on how understandingof Widgets is crucial for Flutter. This chapter will cover some of the basic widgets and some popular widgets that are used when creating an app. Each Widget is explained and given an example of how to use it.

Chapter 4 will cover stateful and stateless widgets. In addition to that, it will give you a better understanding of when and where to use Stateless and Stateful Widgets. This includes code snippet for Stateless and Stateful Widgets.

Chapter 5 will dive deep into the use of Navigator, which is used to move to and back from different screens. This chapter will also shed some light on how to show a popup, or as Flutter says, Model Dialogs.

Chapter 6 is where you can learn about connecting your Flutter app to the database. We will be using Firebase and guide you step-by-step on creating a Firebase project and adding Firebase to Flutter. Next, it will guide you on how to create, read, update and delete data. In addition to that, how to use Listeners to update Realtime.

Chapter 7 will show you how to work with asynchronous programming. This chapter will cover Futures, Awaits, and Async.

Chapter 8 will provide you with an idea about how to organize your data, and how to store data in device memory to be retained even after the app is closed.

Chapter 9 is where you learn about building and releasing the Flutter app. Here you will learn how to change the app name, app icon and manage versioning of the app.

Downloading the code bundles and colored images

Please follow the link to download the
Code Bundles of the book:

https://github.com/OrangeAVA/Ultimate-Flutter-Handbook

The code bundles and images of the book are also hosted on
https://rebrand.ly/215d4d

In case there's an update to the code, it will be updated on the existing GitHub repository.

Errata

We take immense pride in our work at Orange Education Pvt Ltd and follow best practices to ensure the accuracy of our content to provide an indulging reading experience to our subscribers. Our readers are our mirrors, and we use their inputs to reflect and improve upon human errors, if any, that may have occurred during the publishing processes involved. To let us maintain the quality and help us reach out to any readers who might be having difficulties due to any unforeseen errors, please write to us at :

errata@orangeava.com

Your support, suggestions, and feedback are highly appreciated.

DID YOU KNOW

Did you know that Orange Education Pvt Ltd offers eBook versions of every book published, with PDF and ePub files available? You can upgrade to the eBook version at **www.orangeava.com** and as a print book customer, you are entitled to a discount on the eBook copy. Get in touch with us at: **info@orangeava.com** for more details.

At **www.orangeava.com**, you can also read a collection of free technical articles, sign up for a range of free newsletters, and receive exclusive discounts and offers on AVA™ Books and eBooks.

PIRACY

If you come across any illegal copies of our works in any form on the internet, we would be grateful if you would provide us with the location address or website name. Please contact us at **info@orangeava.com** with a link to the material.

ARE YOU INTERESTED IN AUTHORING WITH US?

If there is a topic that you have expertise in, and you are interested in either writing or contributing to a book, please write to us at **business@orangeava.com**. We are on a journey to help developers and tech professionals to gain insights on the present technological advancements and innovations happening across the globe and build a community that believes Knowledge is best acquired by sharing and learning with others. Please reach out to us to learn what our audience demands and how you can be part of this educational reform. We also welcome ideas from tech experts and help them build learning and development content for their domains.

REVIEWS

Please leave a review. Once you have read and used this book, why not leave a review on the site that you purchased it from? Potential readers can then see and use your unbiased opinion to make purchase decisions. We at Orange Education would love to know what you think about our products, and our authors can learn from your feedback. Thank you!

For more information about Orange Education, please visit **www.orangeava.com**.

Table of Contents

CHAPTER 1
Introduction to Flutter

Introduction

Flutter is a powerful, open-source mobile application development framework created by Google. It uses the Dart programming language and offers a variety of features such as a fast development cycle, customizable widgets, and hot reload. The unique architecture of Flutter allows for building high-performance apps for both iOS and Android platforms with a single codebase.

By the end of this chapter, you will have a better understanding of what Flutter can be used for, the benefits of using Flutter and how Flutter architecture works.

Structure

In this chapter, we will cover the following topics:

- Diving into Flutter
- Benefits of using Flutter
- Flutter in real world
- Flutter architecture
- What's next?

Diving into Flutter

Imagine you want to build a native application that has a beautiful interface and runs smoothly on iOS, Android, and the web in a short time frame and low budget. Back in the day, you would have to acquire at least three developers and maintain three different codebases. In addition to that, implementing bug fixes or new features to the application means waiting for three developers to complete their application. Now you might be thinking about how to write this app once and release it to multiple platforms such as iOS, Android, and the web.

Several cross-platform development frameworks have been created to address this issue. A few of the popular ones are Ionic, React Native, Xamarin and Flutter. Out of these, Flutter has been increasing its popularity due to its ability to develop native-like applications in a short period of time and being easy to learn.

Flutter was founded by Google, an open-source mobile UI framework. Flutter uses Dart language to create applications. It supports not just iOS, Android, and the web, but also macOS, Windows, and Linux applications too.

Benefits of using Flutter

Flutter has been gaining popularity among the developing community. Being able to create cross-platform applications is not the only reason why you should consider using Flutter to create your application. Here are some other reasons why you should choose Flutter.

- **Customizable widgets**: Flutter uses widgets to create its UI. Flutter lets you build your own custom widgets which enables you to create flexible and beautiful UI. This gives the developer full control over how each element is seen and behaves on the screen.
- **Hot reload and hot restart feature**: One of the best features that Flutter brings to the table is the hot reload and hot restart feature. It enables the developer to see the results or test instantaneously without having to terminate and re-run the build every time a new feature is added, removed or even when a bug is fixed. This helps to reduce the build time significantly and increase the productivity of the developer. You can rebuild the widget tree by hot reloading while the hot restart feature can be used in an instance where major changes are done to the code and/ or if the state needs to be reset.
- **Small learning curve**: Under the hood, Flutter uses Dart to build its apps. Dart is a very simple programming language that has been created by Google to compete with JavaScript (JS).

- **Ability to maintain a single code base**: Since Flutter allows you to develop cross-platform apps, you don't have to maintain multiple source codes.
- **Reduced development time and cost**: Flutter can cut down the development time to half compared to the use of native technologies. Therefore, it will reduce the cost of hiring multiple developers and reduce labor hours as well as time to release a fully functional app.
- **Native-like performance**: Flutter's ability to compile code into native like code for all the platforms will allow the developers to create high-performance applications in the native language. It offers faster development, better performance, and more flexibility.
- **Having good documentation and community support**: Having good documentation and community support for technology is essential for its success. Flutter, backed up by Google, not only has great documentation, but it also has an incredibly active community that is always willing to help new developers who are just getting started with Flutter development. This makes it easier for developers to ask questions or find solutions when they run into problems while developing their apps.

Flutter in real world

Flutter is a versatile and powerful framework that can be used to create a wide range of mobile apps, including but not limited to:

- **E-commerce apps**: Flutter's widgets and animations make it easy to create visually appealing and interactive e-commerce apps.
- **Social media apps**: The framework's support for real-time data and web sockets makes it a great choice for building social media apps.
- **Gaming apps**: Flutter's high performance and support for 2D and 3D animations make it a great choice for developing mobile games.
- **Business apps**: Flutter's ability to create custom widgets and its support for offline data storage make it a great choice for building business apps.
- **Educational apps**: Flutter's ability to create visually appealing and interactive apps makes it a great choice for building educational apps.
- **Travel apps**: The framework's ability to access native features and integrate with Google Maps makes it a great choice for building travel apps.
- **IoT and connected devices**: Flutter has great support for building apps for IoT and connected devices, thanks to its ability to communicate with Bluetooth and other low-level APIs.

- **Dashboard and Monitoring apps**: Flutter's ability to create custom widgets and its support for real-time data make it a great choice for building monitoring and dashboard apps.
- **Healthcare apps**: The framework's ability to access native features such as camera and microphone make it a great choice for building healthcare apps.
- **Mapping and Navigation apps**: Flutter's ability to integrate with Google Maps and other mapping services makes it a great choice for building navigation apps.

This list is not exhaustive, and Flutter can be used to create many other types of apps that are not mentioned here. Thanks to its expressive and flexible design, Flutter allows developers to create a wide variety of apps that are fast, responsive, and visually attractive.

Flutter architecture

Flutter is a layered architecture that helps developers create beautiful and expressive applications for mobile, web, and desktop platforms. It uses a layered approach which makes it easier for developers to create apps quickly and efficiently. The layers include the Framework layer, Engine layer, and Embedder layer (*Figure 1.1*).

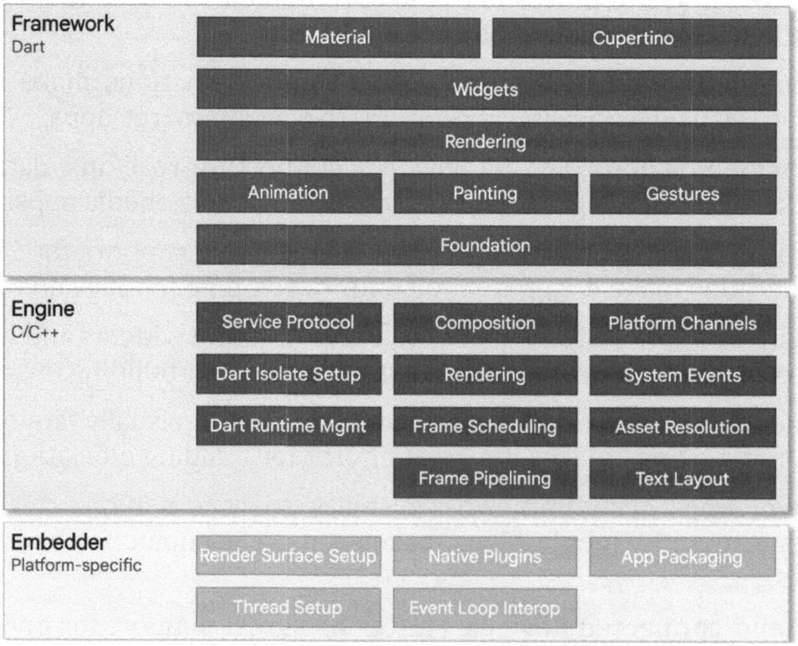

***Figure 1.1**: Flutter Architectural Layers*
(https://docs.Flutter.dev/resources/architectural-overview)

Framework Layer

The Framework is the layer that sits on top among the three layers. It provides the basic building blocks of an application such as widgets, rending, animation, layout, and gestures. The core functionality of the framework, including the widget tree, the rendering engine, and the Dart runtime. It also provides the basic building blocks for creating an app, such as the Stateful Widget and Stateless Widget classes.

The core of the Flutter architecture is the use of widgets. A widget in Flutter represents a visual element of an app, such as a button or a text field. Widgets are not just simple UI elements, however; they also contain logic and state. This allows for a highly modular and reusable codebase, as well as easy management of the app's state. The Flutter framework also includes several built-in widgets and other tools that make it easy to create beautiful, responsive apps with minimal effort. For example, the Material library provides a set of widgets that are based on Google's Material Design guidelines, and the Cupertino library provides a set of widgets that are based on Apple's iOS design guidelines. Additionally, Flutter includes a powerful layout engine that makes it easy to create complex, responsive UI with minimal code.

Engine Layer

The engine layer is built on top of the Impeller graphics library, which provides a high-performance 2D rendering engine. Impeller is used to draw the widgets and other elements that make up a Flutter app, and it also handles tasks such as compositing and GPU acceleration.

The engine layer also includes a Dart runtime, which is used to execute the Dart code that powers a Flutter app. The Dart runtime is responsible for handling the execution of the app's code, as well as managing its memory and resources.

The engine layer also includes a set of C++ bindings, which provide a bridge between the Dart code and the native platform. These bindings allow the app to access platform-specific features, such as the camera or the device's sensors, and they also provide a way for the app to handle platform-specific events, such as touch input or notifications.

One of the key benefits of the engine layer is its ability to provide a consistent, high-performance experience across multiple platforms. Because the engine layer is written in C++, it can be easily ported to different platforms, such as Android and iOS. This allows a single codebase to be used to create apps for multiple platforms, which can significantly reduce the development time and costs.

Embedder Layer

The embedder layer is responsible for providing the necessary bindings and APIs to run the Flutter engine on a specific platform. It provides the necessary hooks to the host platform's windowing system, input system, and other native services. This allows the Flutter engine to access the platform-specific features and resources it needs to run the app.

One of the key responsibilities of the embedder layer is to create the necessary environment for the Flutter engine to run. This includes creating the window for the app to run in, as well as handling the input and output events. The embedder layer also manages the app's lifecycle and handles platform-specific events, such as push notifications or background tasks.

he embedder layer also includes a set of APIs that allow the Flutter app to interact with the host platform. These APIs provide access to platform-specific features, such as the camera or sensors, as well as services such as in-app purchases or push notifications.

The embedder layer is written in C++, and it's designed to be platform-specific, meaning that a different implementation of the embedder layer is required for each platform. This allows the Flutter engine to be easily ported to different platforms and provides a consistent experience across multiple platforms.

The layered architecture of Flutter allows for a clear separation of concerns between different parts of the framework, which makes it easy to understand and maintain. The architecture is also designed to be highly modular, which allows for easy customization and extensibility.

In summary, Flutter is a well-designed framework that uses a layered architecture to separate concerns between different parts of the framework. The main layers of the architecture are the engine layer, the embedder layer, the framework layer, and the application layer. This allows for a clear separation of concerns, making the framework easy to understand and maintain, and also easy to customize and extend.

Up next

In the following chapters, we will focus on the application layer, where you will learn how to implement the business logic and behavior of your app. We will cover topics such as state management, data persistence, and networking.

Finally, we will explore how to deploy your app to the different platforms and how to handle platform-specific features. We will also cover some tips and best practices for debugging and optimizing your app.

At the end of the book, you will be able to create a fully functional, high-performance app using Flutter and be able to take on more complex projects in the future.

Conclusion

Flutter is a powerful, open-source mobile application development framework created by Google. It uses the Dart programming language and offers a variety of features such as a fast development cycle, customizable widgets, and hot reload. Its unique architecture allows for building high-performance apps for iOS, Android, MacOS, Windows, and Linux platforms with a single codebase. Overall, Flutter is a great option for developers looking to create visually stunning, high-performing mobile apps.

The next chapter will cover what you need to start your Flutter development journey. Moreover, it will guide you on how to set up your development environment, creating and running your first Flutter app. Furthermore, it will give you a good understanding of Flutter folder structure and how to add assets such as images to your Flutter app.

Points to Remember

- Flutter is an open-source mobile application development framework created by Google.
- It uses the Dart programming language.
- Flutter offers a fast development cycle and customizable widgets.
- It has a hot reload feature, which allows developers to see changes made in the code instantly in the app.
- Flutter's architecture allows for building high-performance apps for both iOS and Android platforms with a single codebase.
- Flutter is the most-suitable for creating visually stunning and high-performing mobile apps.
- With Flutter, developers can build apps for web, mobile, desktop, and more.

Multiple Choice Questions

1. **What programming language is used in Flutter?**
   a. JavaScript
   b. Python
   c. Dart
   d. C#

2. **What is the main purpose of Flutter's "hot reload" feature?**
   a. To improve app performance
   b. To fix bugs in the code
   c. To instantly see changes made in the code
   d. To make app more responsive

3. **What type of apps can be built with Flutter?**
   a. Mobile apps for iOS and Android
   b. Web apps
   c. Desktop apps
   d. All of the above

4. **What is the advantage of using Flutter's architecture?**
   a. Building high performance apps for iOS and Android platforms
   b. Building apps for web and desktop
   c. Creating visually stunning apps
   d. All of the above

5. **Is Flutter an open-source framework?**
   a. Yes
   b. No
   c. Partially owned by google

6. **What is the main advantage of using Flutter?**
   a. Single Codebase
   b. Customizable widgets
   c. Fast development cycle
   d. All of the above

Answers

1. c
2. c
3. d
4. d
5. a
6. d

CHAPTER 2
Getting Started

Introduction

Welcome to the world of Flutter! In this chapter, we will be introducing you to the basics of Flutter, a popular open-source framework for developing mobile applications. You'll learn how to set up your development environment, create a new project, and build your first app with Flutter. We'll also take a brief look at the key concepts and features of the framework, such as the use of widgets and the Dart programming language. By the end of this chapter, you'll have a solid foundation for building your own apps with Flutter.

We'll start by discussing the requirements for setting up a Flutter development environment, including installing the Flutter SDK and any necessary dependencies. We'll walk you through the process of creating a new project, including configuring the project settings and creating the basic structure of the app.

Finally, we'll build a simple "Hello, World!" app together, which will give you a hands-on introduction to the basics of building an app with Flutter. By the end of this chapter, you'll have a solid foundation for building your own apps with Flutter and be ready to dive deeper into the framework in future chapters.

So, let's get started! With this guide, you will be able to create your first mobile application, and you will be able to understand the basics of the framework.

By the end of this chapter, you will have a clear understanding of how to start building your own Flutter application.

Structure

In this chapter, we will cover the following topics:

- Requirements
- Getting the development environment ready
- Creating your first Flutter app
- Running your first Flutter app
- Understanding folder structure
- Adding assets

Requirements

In order to run Flutter and build mobile apps, there are a few system requirements that need to be met. These include:

- **Operating System:** Flutter can be run on Windows, Mac, or Linux.
- **Hardware:** A machine with min. 8GB (recommended 16GB) of RAM, which is recommended, and a recent 64-bit CPU is required to run Flutter.
- **Disk Space:** You will need between 600 MB to 2.8GB of available disk space to install Flutter depending on your Operating System (OS).
- **Software:** You will need to have a recent version of Git, the Android SDK and/or Xcode, and an IDE or code editor of your choice installed on your computer.
- **Dart SDK:** You will also need to have the Dart SDK installed, as Flutter uses the Dart programming language for developing apps.
- **Emulator or physical device:** You will need to have an Android emulator or iOS simulator to run the app, or a physical device connected to your machine to test the app on it.
- **PATH environment variable:** You will need to add the Flutter SDK to your PATH environment variable so that you can access the command-line tools from any directory.

By meeting these requirements, you'll be able to run Flutter and start building mobile apps for Android and iOS. It's important to keep in mind that as you dive deeper into the framework, additional requirements may arise, so it's always a good idea to check the documentation of the packages you are using and the official website for the latest requirements.

Getting the development environment ready

Let us start diving into the world of Flutter by getting your development environment ready.

Step 1: Installing the Flutter SDK

a. **Getting Flutter SDK**

The first step is to download and install the Flutter SDK from the official website (**https://flutter.dev/docs/get-started/install**). The process of installing the Flutter SDK is relatively straightforward and can be done in a few simple steps:

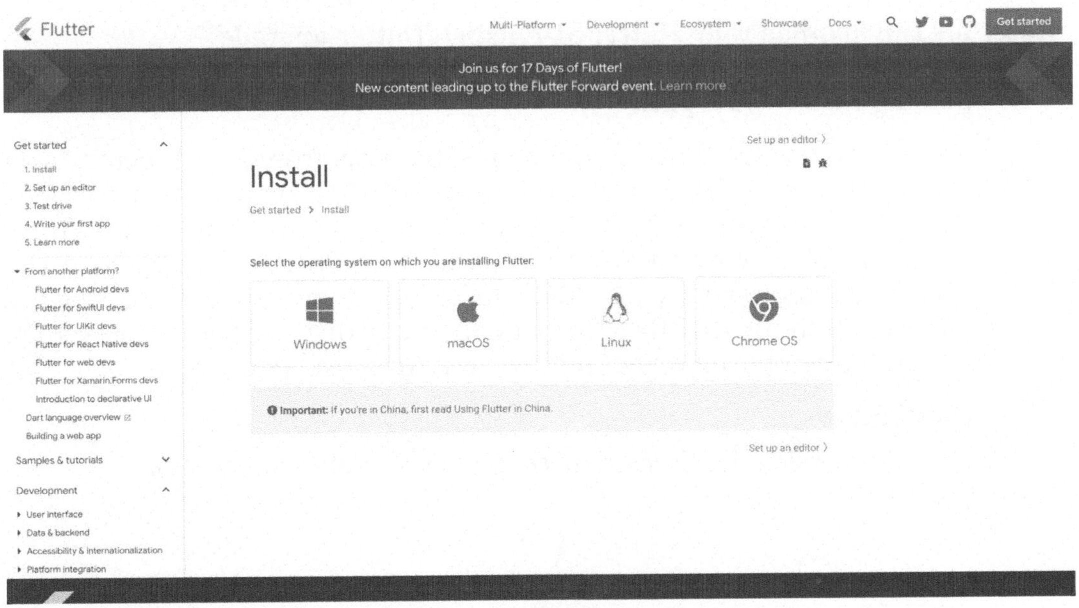

Figure 2.1: *Flutter Install page* (**https://flutter.dev/docs/get-started/install**)

As shown in *Figure* 2.1, you will be greeted with this page. Select your OS and it will take show you the OS-related download link. From there, scroll down to "Get the Flutter SDK" and download the latest stable release of Flutter SDK as shown in *Figure* 2.2.

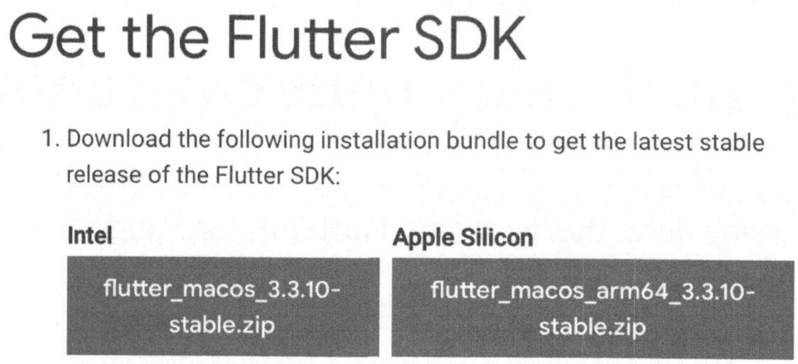

***Figure* 2.2**: *Get the Flutter SDK (macOS binary)*

After downloading your stable version of Flutter, extract it to a directory that you are comfortable with. This directory will be the location where your Flutter SDK will reside.

Note: *You can upgrade your Flutter SDK using "flutter upgrade"*

b. **Setting Flutter SDK path**

In order to use the Flutter command-line tools from any directory, you will need to add the Flutter SDK to your PATH environment variable. Exporting the PATH to Flutter allows you to run Flutter commands from the terminal or command prompt, without having to navigate to the specific directory where the SDK is located. The process of exporting the PATH to Flutter is slightly different depending on your operating system, so here's a brief overview of how to do it for each one:

On Windows:

1. Right-click the *Start* icon, then click System (*Figure* 2.3).

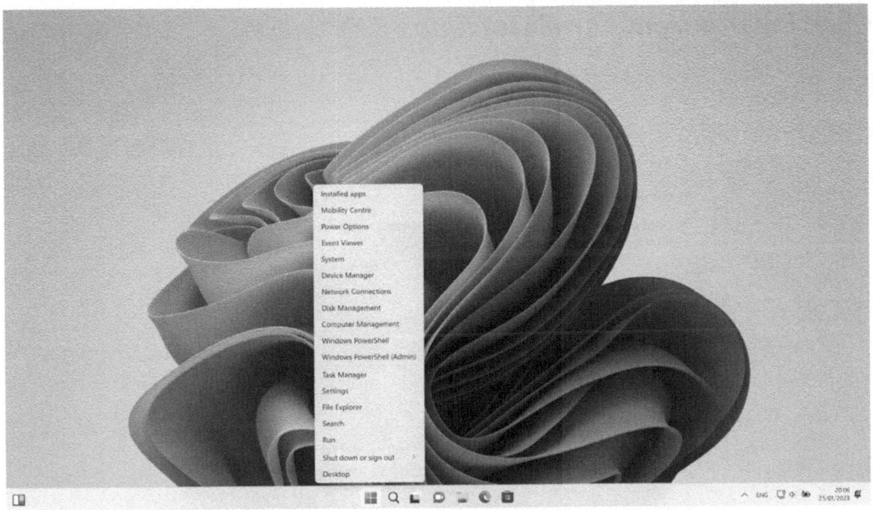

Figure 2.3: Windows

2. Click *Advanced system settings* (*Figure 2.4*).

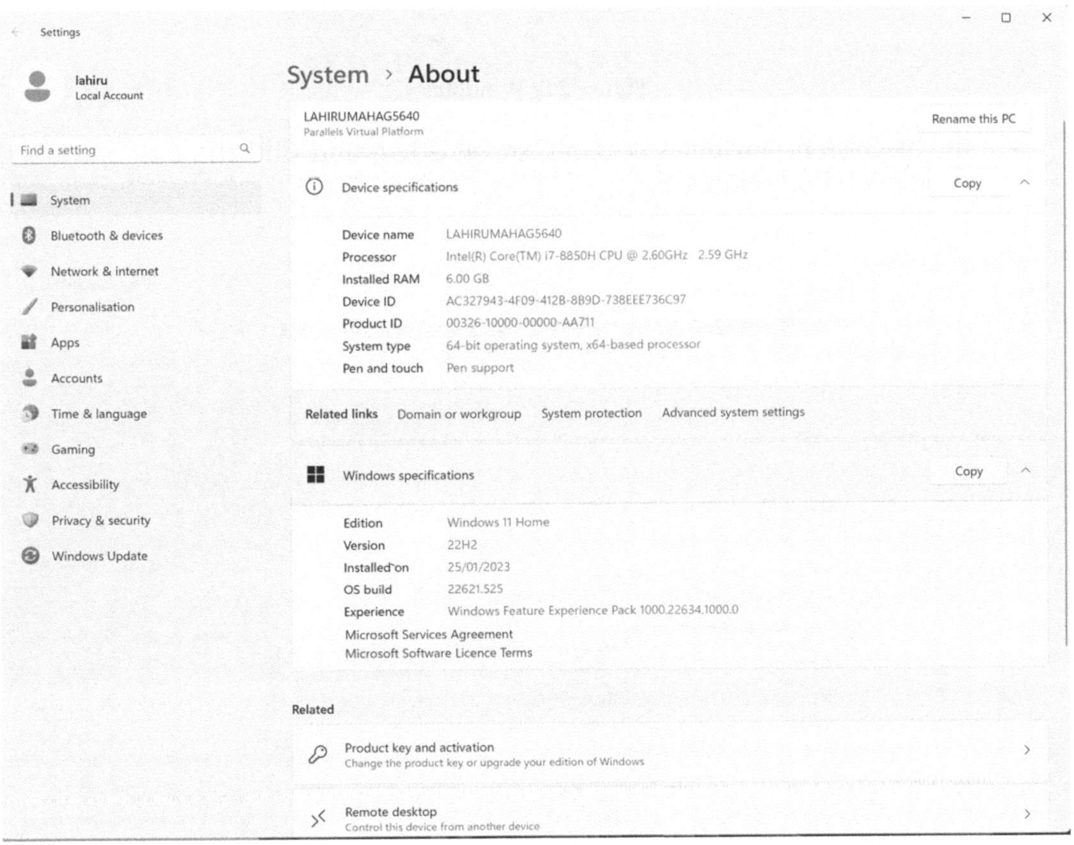

Figure 2.4: Windows

3. Click *Environment Variables* (*Figure 2.5*).

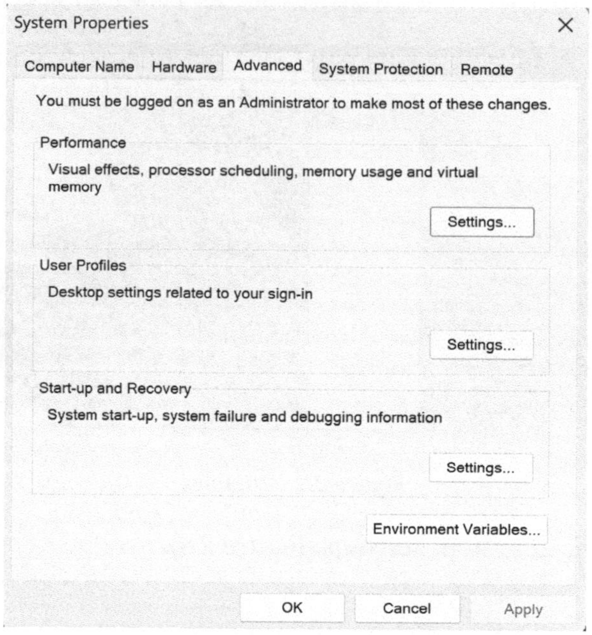

Figure 2.5: *Windows*

4. In the *System Variables* section, scroll down and find the *Path variable*, then click *Edit* (*Figure 2.6*).

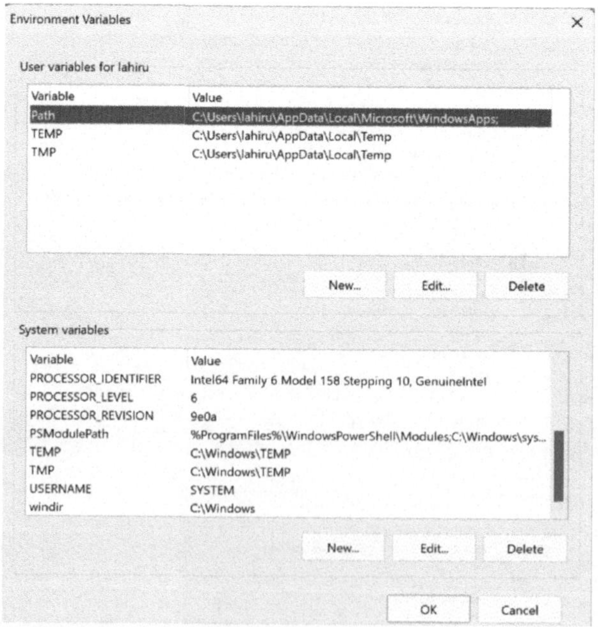

Figure 2.6: *Windows*

5. Click *New* and enter the path of the Flutter SDK's bin directory, for example, (*Figure* 2.7): C:\src\flutter\bin

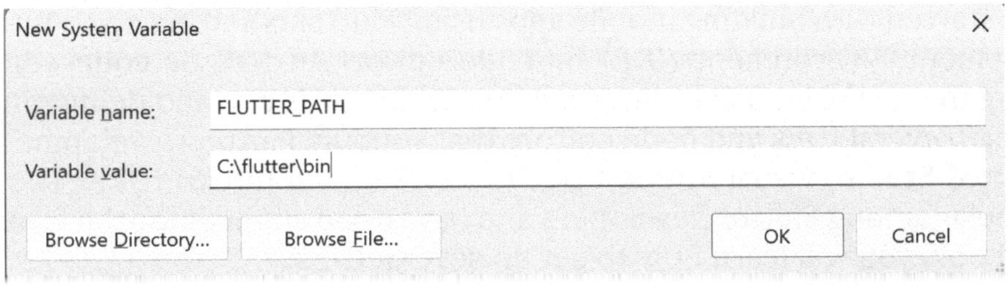

***Figure* 2.7**: *Windows*

6. Click OK on all three dialogs in the following order *Figure* 2.7> *Figure* 2.6 > *Figure* 2.5.
7. Restart any command prompt or terminal window for the changes to take effect.

On Mac and Linux:

1. Open a *terminal* window and enter the command "*nano ~/.bash_profile*".
2. Add the path of the Flutter SDK's bin directory to the file, for example, export PATH="$PATH:~/development/flutter/bin"
3. Press *Cmd*+O (*Ctrl*+O) and *enter* to save the changes and *Cmd*+X (*Ctrl*+X) to exit the nano editor
4. Reload the *terminal* with the command "*source ~/.bash_profile*".

Note: Depending on your system, you may need to restart any open terminal or command prompt windows for the changes to take effect. Additionally, keep in mind that if you move the Flutter SDK to a different location, you will need to update the PATH accordingly.

Once you have completed these steps, the path to the Flutter SDK will be exported and you will be able to access the command-line tools provided by the SDK from any directory on your machine. You can test this by running the command ***"flutter doctor"*** in a terminal or command prompt, which will check your system to make sure that all the necessary dependencies are installed and that your environment is ready for development.

Tip: You can use "flutter doctor" to check issues, look for the status of connected devices, status of development IDE, environment version and updates.

Step 2: Setting up an IDE

Once you have installed the Flutter SDK and exported the path, the next step in getting started with building mobile apps using Flutter is setting up an Integrated Development Environment (IDE) or code editor. An IDE or code editor is a program that provides a user interface for writing, editing, and debugging code. There are several IDEs and code editors that support Flutter development, such as Android Studio, Visual Studio Code (VS Code), and IntelliJ IDEA. These IDEs are popular among Flutter developers and have good support for the framework. In this book, you will learn how to set up several IDEs.

This book will guide you on how to install Android Studio, VS Code and Xcode. We will be using VS Code for our development process. Even though Xcode is not used to develop Flutter, it is a development environment for macOS that is required to run Flutter apps on iOS devices or simulators. Xcode is needed because it contains the necessary tools for building and signing iOS apps, including the iOS Simulator and the iOS SDK. When you run a Flutter app on an iOS device or simulator, the Flutter framework uses the XCode tools to build the app into an iOS bundle (a .ipa file) and then signs it with a provisioning profile and signing certificate. This is necessary to ensure that the app can be installed and run on an iOS device.

Android Studio

Android Studio is an Integrated Development Environment (IDE) that can be used for building mobile apps using the Flutter framework. It is the officially recommended IDE for developing Flutter apps for Android and provides a number of features that can make developing Flutter apps easier, such as a visual layout editor, debugging tools, and performance testing tools.

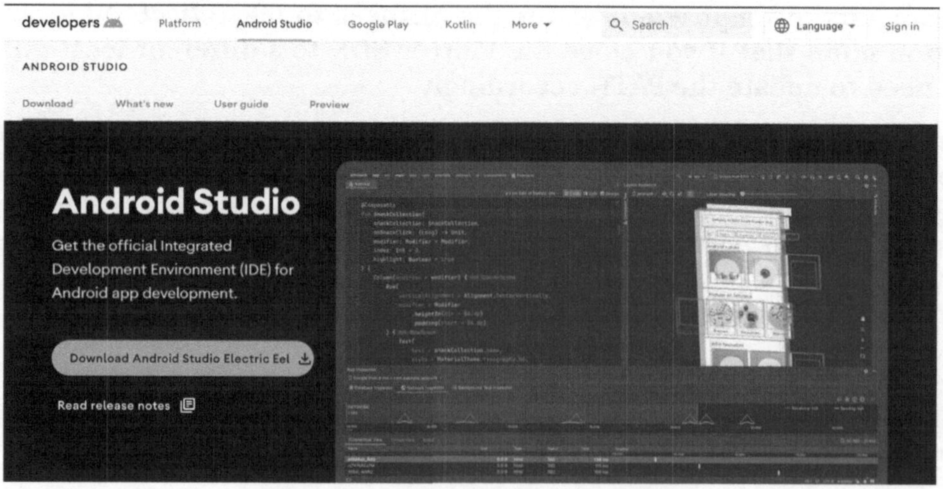

Figure 2.8: *Android Studio home page*

Note: Having Java Development Kit (JDK) is a must to run the Android Studio. You can download the JDK from the Oracle website (https://www.oracle.com/au/java/technologies/downloads/).

By following these steps, you will have Android Studio installed and configured for Flutter development, and you will be able to start building Android apps with the framework:

1. Go to the official Android Studio website (**https://developer.android.com/studio/**) and download the latest version of Android Studio for your operating system.
2. Once the download is complete, run the installer and follow the instructions to install Android Studio on your computer.
3. Once Android Studio is installed, open it and go to the *Plugins* menu. Search for "Flutter by flutter.dev" and "Dart by JetBrains s.r.o." and *install* plugins (*Figure* 2.9).

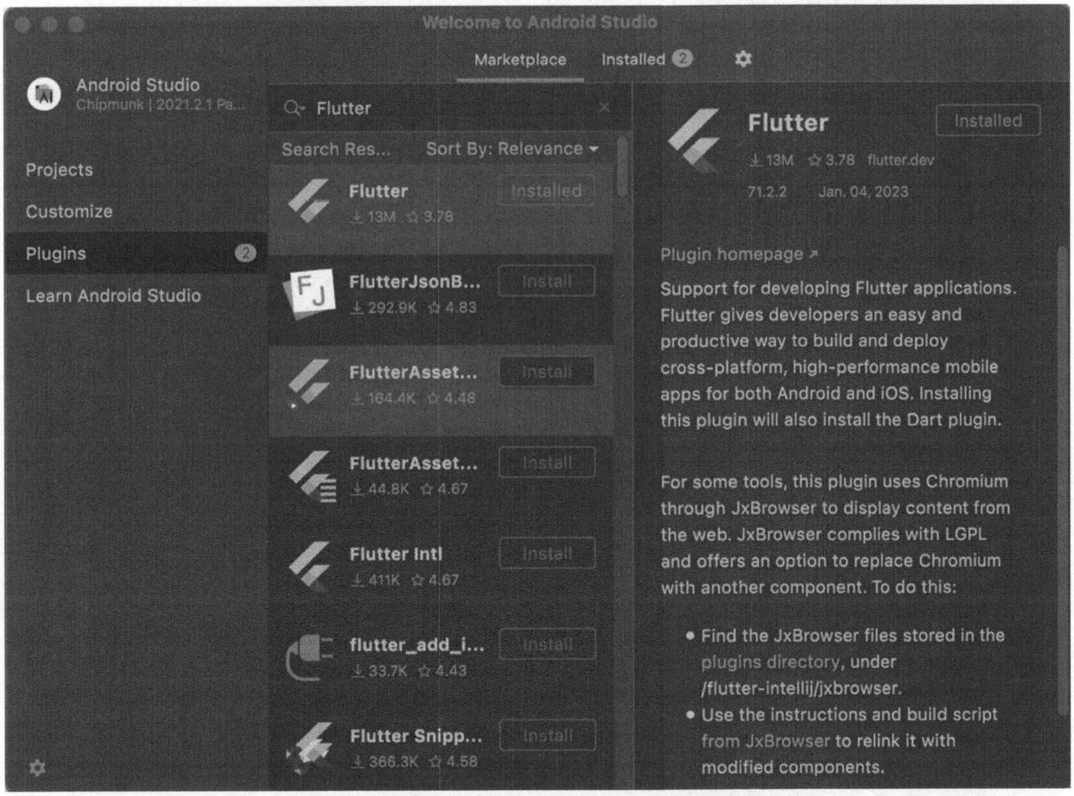

***Figure* 2.9**: *Android Studio plugins menu* - iOS

4. Go to the *Preferences* or *Settings* menu, and then to *Appearance & Behavior > System Settings > Android SDK* section (*Figure 2.10*).

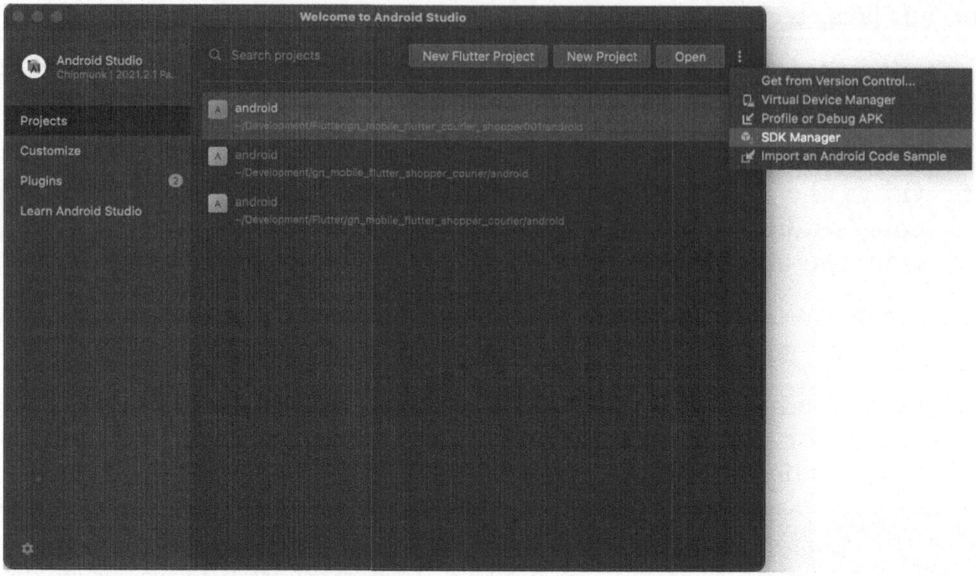

Figure 2.10: *Android Studio – Accessing SDK Manager*

5. Click on the SDK *Platforms* tab and select the latest version of Android (*Figure 2.11*).

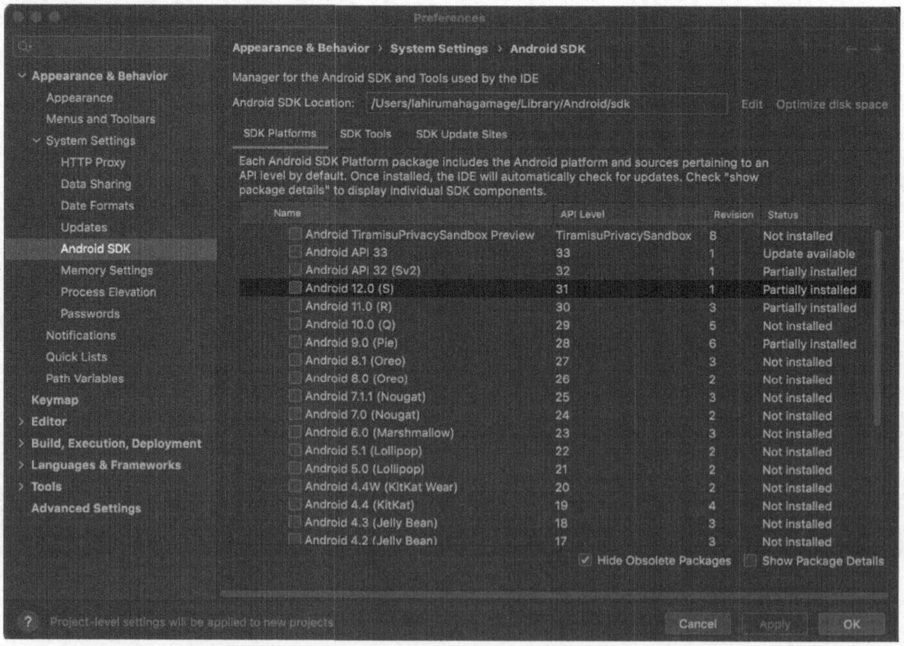

Figure 2.11: *Android Studio – Getting the latest android*

6. Next, click on the SDK *Tools* tab and select the *Android SDK Command-line tools* that you need (*Figure* 2.12).

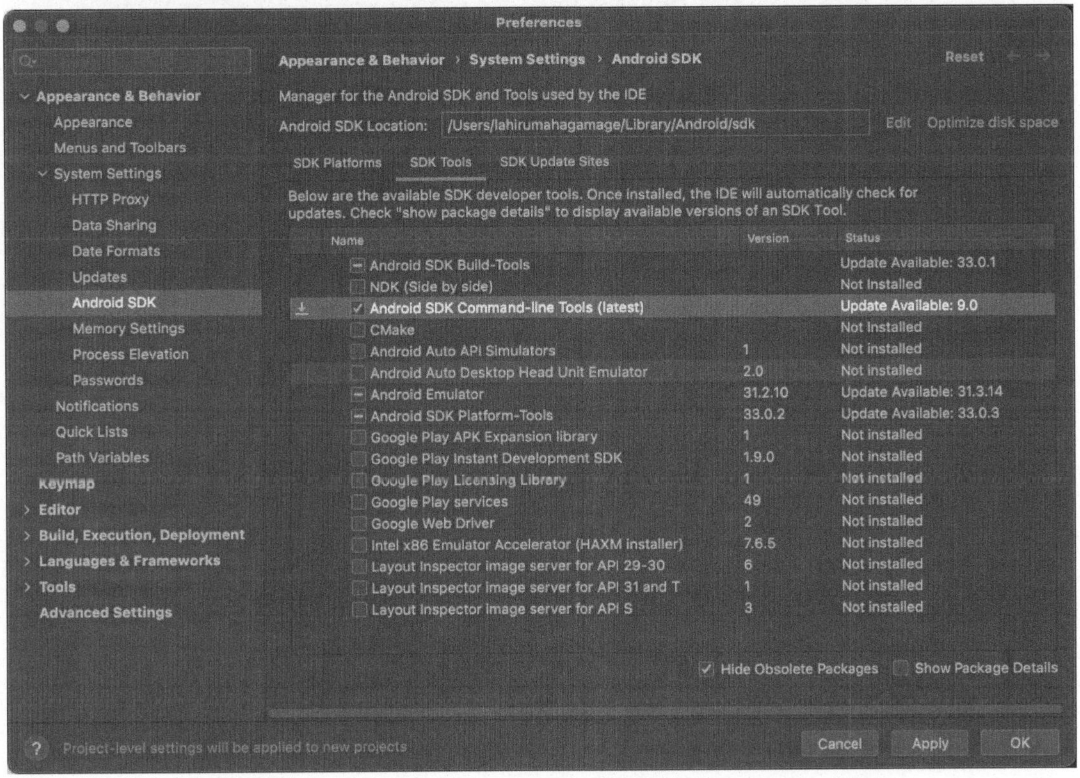

Figure 2.12: *Android Studio – Android SDK Command Line Tools*

Remember that, depending on the features you want to implement, additional setup may be required, so it's always a good idea to check the documentation of the packages you are using for the latest requirements.

Xcode

Installing Xcode is an essential step for developing iOS and macOS applications using Flutter. We will walk you through the process of installing Xcode on your Mac and setting it up for Flutter development.

Before we begin, it's important to note that Xcode is only available for Mac and is not supported on Windows or Linux. Additionally, Xcode is a large application, so it may take some time to download and install, depending on your internet connection.

Follow these steps to install Xcode:

1. Open the *App Store* on your Mac.

2. Search for "Xcode" in the search bar (*Figure* 2.13).

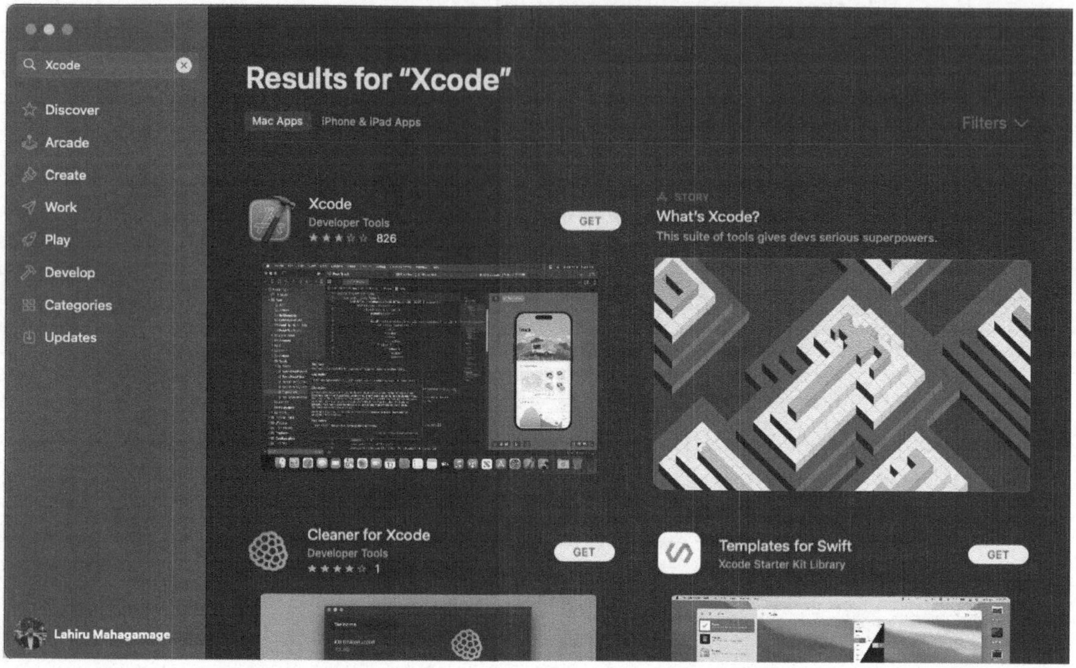

Figure 2.13: *App Store – result for the search "Xcode"*

3. Step 3: Click on the *Get* button to start the download and installation process.
4. Once the installation is complete, you'll find Xcode in the *Applications* folder on your mac.
5. Open Xcode and accept the license agreement.
6. Xcode will then perform any additional setup and installation.
7. Install command-line tools by running the command "*xcode-select – install*" in the *terminal.*

Now that you have Xcode installed, you can start developing iOS and macOS applications using Flutter. Xcode provides a comprehensive suite of tools for developing, testing, and debugging your applications. With its intuitive user interface, you can easily design and build your apps with the help of drag-and-drop tools and visual editors.

It's important to keep in mind that Xcode is updated regularly by Apple, so it's a good idea to keep your installation up to date to ensure optimal performance and compatibility with the latest features of Flutter.

Visual Studio Code (VS Code)

Visual Studio Code (VS Code) is a popular code editor that is widely used for developing applications using Flutter, which is a free and open-source code editor developed by Microsoft and is available for Windows, Mac, and Linux. It provides a comprehensive suite of tools and features that make it an ideal choice for Flutter development.

One of the key features of VS Code is its IntelliSense, which provides code completion, parameter info, and other helpful hints as you write your code. This makes it easier to write accurate and efficient code. VS Code also provides a built-in code debugger, which allows you to step through your code, set breakpoints, and inspect variables. This makes it easier to find and fix bugs in your code.

Another important feature of VS Code for Flutter development is its visual editors. These editors allow you to design and build your apps using a visual interface, rather than having to write code by hand. This can be especially useful for designers and developers who are new to Flutter. In addition, VS Code also provides a wide range of extensions such as Flutter, Dart, YAML, Pubspec Assist, Prettier and more that can be installed to enhance its functionality. The Flutter extension, for example, provides a set of tools and features specifically designed for Flutter development, including a visual layout editor, a Dart code formatter, and a Flutter outline view. The following figure shows the VS Code home page.

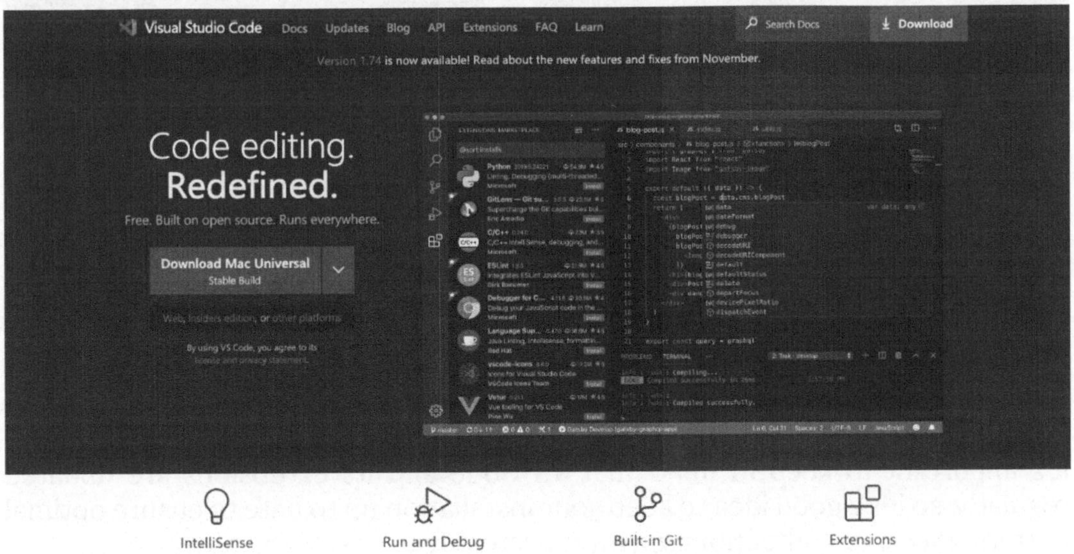

Figure 2.14: *Visual Studio Code Home Page* (**https://code.visualstudio.com**)

The following are the simple steps that you can follow to install VS Code:

1. Download the latest version of VS Code from the official website (***https://code.visualstudio.com***).
2. Once the download is complete, open the installer and follow the prompts to install VS Code.
3. Once the installation is complete, open VS Code.
4. Click on the *Extensions* button on the left sidebar or press *Cmd+Shift+X* (*Ctrl+Shift+X*) to open the *Extensions* pane.
5. Search for the *Flutter* extension and click on the *install* button to install it (*Figure 2.15*).

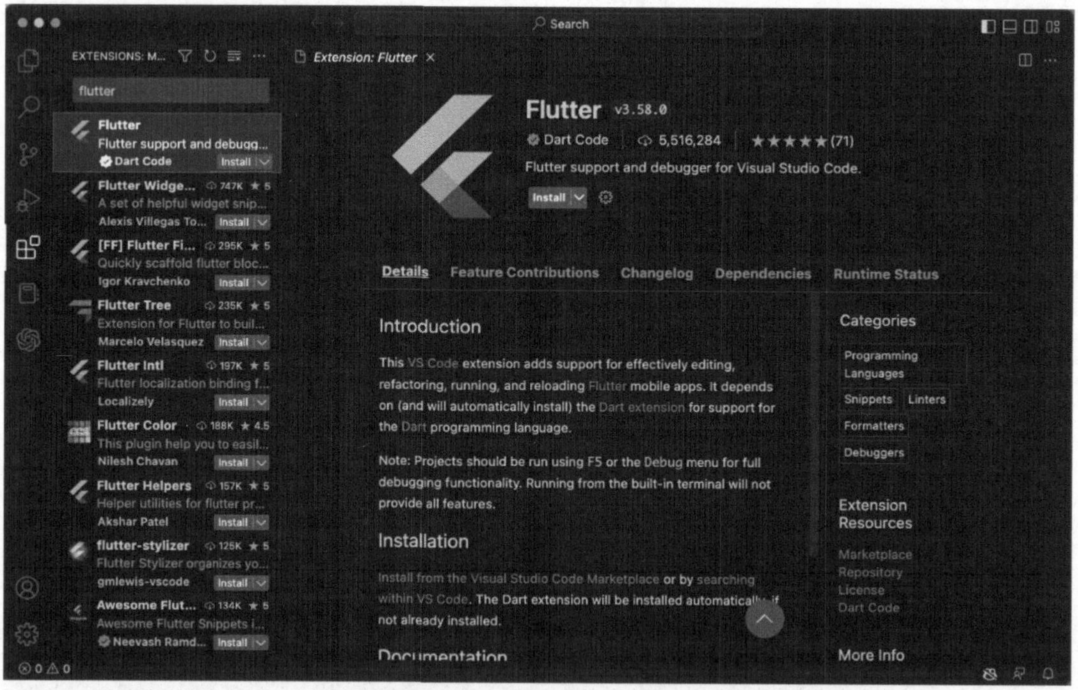

***Figure 2.15**: Flutter extension in VS Code*

It's important to keep in mind that VS Code and its extensions are updated regularly, so it's a good idea to keep your installation up to date to ensure optimal performance and compatibility with the latest features of Flutter.

Now that you have installed everything needed, you can start developing applications using Flutter. Before starting our development, let us confirm there are no issues with our environment, and everything is working the way it needs to be. To do that run "*flutter doctor*". There should not be any issues as shown in

Figure 2.15. If there are any issues, these should be rectified before starting your development journey.

```
> flutter doctor
Doctor summary (to see all details, run flutter doctor -v):
[✓] Flutter (Channel stable, 3.3.10, on macOS 13.1 22C65 darwin-arm, locale en-AU)
[✓] Android toolchain - develop for Android devices (Android SDK version 33.0.0)
[✓] Xcode - develop for iOS and macOS (Xcode 14.2)
[✓] Chrome - develop for the web
[✓] Android Studio (version 2021.2)
[✓] VS Code (version 1.74.3)
[✓] Connected device (3 available)
[✓] HTTP Host Availability

• No issues found!
```

***Figure* 2.16**: *Flutter doctor on Terminal*

Next, we will see how to create our first application using Flutter. Even though there is no set IDE for the development of Flutter throughout this book VS code will be used. Ultimately, the choice of IDE will depend on your personal preferences and what you are most comfortable with. Each of the IDEs mentioned above has its own set of pros and cons, so it's best to try them out and see which one you like the most.

Creating your first Flutter app

Now, you have configured our Flutter development environment successfully on our device. Let us create our first Flutter app. There are a couple of ways to do this, but in this book, you will learn the following:

1. **Terminal/CMD**
   a. Open terminal/cmd.
   b. Go to the directory where the project needs to be saved.
   c. Run the command "*flutter create <name_of_the_project>*". E.g., *flutter create hello_world*
   d. Your first Flutter project has now been created.

2. **VS Code**
   a. Open VS Code.

b. Press *Cmd+Shift+P* (*Ctrl+Shift+P*) and search *flutter new project* and select *Application* (*Figure 2.17*).

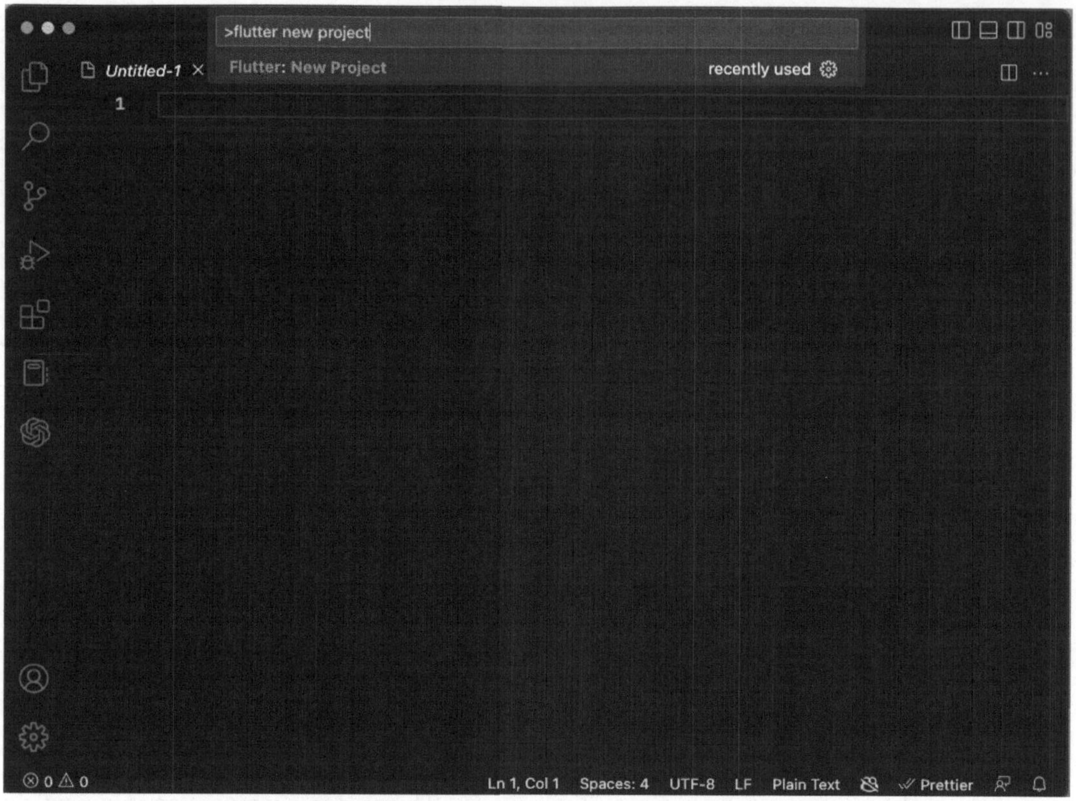

Figure 2.17*: Creating a new Flutter project in VS Code*

c. Select a directory to create your project and enter your project name. *E.g., hello_world*

Tip: When naming a flutter project always use snake_case. Snake case refers to the style of writing in which each space is replaced with an underscore character, and the first letter of each word is written in lowercase.

d. Finally, press **Enter** and wait till the project is created (*Figure 2.18* shows final outcome)

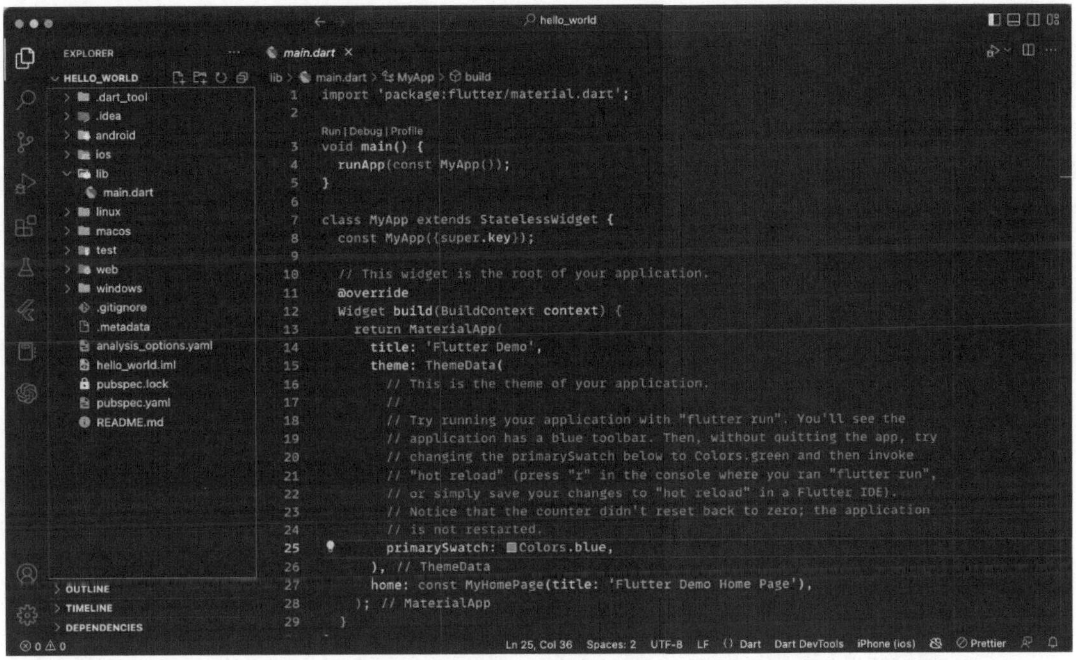

Figure 2.18: *New project*

Understanding folder structure

We'll explore the folder structure of the Flutter project. Understanding the folder structure of a Flutter project is important as it helps to organize your code, assets and resources in a clear and efficient manner.

The root folder of the Flutter project contains the following main directories:

- **lib**: This is the main directory for your Flutter code. It contains Dart files for your application's logic, UI, and assets.
- **build**: Contains the compiled output of your Flutter app. When you run your Flutter project using the flutter run command or build it for specific platforms using flutter build, Flutter compiles your Dart code into platform-specific code (e.g., Android APK or iOS IPA) and places the resulting files in the build folder.
- **assets**: This directory contains all the assets that are used by the application, such as images and fonts.
- **pubspec.yaml**: This is the main configuration file for your Flutter project. It contains information about your project's dependencies, assets, and other configurations.

- **ios**: This directory contains all the necessary files for building an iOS app, including the Xcode project, storyboards, and app icons.
- **android**: This directory contains all the necessary files for building an Android app, including the AndroidManifest.xml file, Gradle files, and app icons.
- **test**: This directory contains test files for your Flutter application. These files test your application's logic, UI, and assets.

The lib directory is the most important directory in your Flutter project. It contains all the Dart codes for your application. By convention, it contains a few subdirectories, including:

- **main.dart**: This is the main entry point of your Flutter application. It contains the main function that launches the application.
- **widgets**: This directory contains all the custom widgets that you have created for your Flutter application.
- **models**: This directory contains the model classes for your Flutter application, including any data models or domain models that you have created.
- **services**: This directory contains any services or APIs that your Flutter application uses, such as authentication or data storage.

Understanding the folder structure of a Flutter project is important to help you organize your code, assets, and resources. By convention, Flutter projects have a well-defined structure that includes directories for code, assets, and configuration files. With a clear understanding of the folder structure, you can build Flutter applications that are well-organized, maintainable, and scalable.

Running your first Flutter app

Once you have completed the preceding steps, it's time to run it on an emulator or a physical device as follows:

Note: If you have a physical device, it needs to be connected prior to running your Flutter project

1. **Terminal/CMD**
    a. Open terminal/cmd.
    b. Go to the directory where the project needs to be saved.

c. Run the command **flutter emulators**. This will show a list of available emulators which shows the emulator id, emulator name, manufacturer and OS (*Figure 2.19*).

```
❯ flutter emulators
2 available emulators:

apple_ios_simulator • iOS Simulator   • Apple  • ios
Pixel_5_API_33      • Pixel 5 API 33 • Google • android
```

Figure 2.19: *Emulators available in the System*

d. Run command **flutter emulators --launch <emulator_id>** , for example, **flutter emulators -launch apple_ios_simulator**

e. Once the simulator is open, run the command **flutter run**. If you have more than one device, it will prompt you to choose the device (*Figure 2.20*).

```
❯ flutter run
Multiple devices found:
iPhone (mobile)            • 00008030-001E38583C46802E             • ios
• iOS 16.1.1 20B101
iPhone 14 Pro Max (mobile) • 362DED1A-DE39-4B05-9FA5-7E2557CB8848 • ios
• com.apple.CoreSimulator.SimRuntime.iOS-16-2 (simulator)
macOS (desktop)            • macos                                 • darwin-arm64
• macOS 13.1 22C65 darwin-arm (Rosetta)
Chrome (web)               • chrome                                •
web-javascript • Google Chrome 109.0.5414.119
[1]: iPhone (00008030-001E38583C46802E)
[2]: iPhone 14 Pro Max (362DED1A-DE39-4B05-9FA5-7E2557CB8848)
[3]: macOS (macos)
[4]: Chrome (chrome)
Please choose one (To quit, press "q/Q"): 2
Launching lib/main.dart on iPhone 14 Pro Max in debug mode...
```

Figure 2.20: *Running the project*

2. **VS Code**
   a. Open terminal/cmd.
   b. Go to the directory where the project needs to be saved.
   c. To open the directory on VS Code, run the command **code**.

d. Then press *Cmd+Shift+P* (*Ctrl+Shift+P*) and search for **Launch Emulator** (*Figure 2.21*).

***Figure 2.21**: Launching emulator from VS Code*

e. Once the emulator is up and running, select the device by clicking on the device selector.

f. Then, click on **Run** > Start **Debugging** or F5.

Congratulations! You've completed the journey of running your first Flutter app. You have now explored the basics of the Flutter framework and learned how to create a simple application.

Adding assets

Flutter is a great platform for developing mobile applications and it is even better now that it supports adding assets. With the addition of asset support, we can now use images, videos, audio, fonts, and other files within our Flutter apps. This opens up a whole new level of possibilities when it comes to creating visually stunning and interactive apps.

To add assets to Flutter, first, add **assets** inside the Flutter project root and then use the pubspec.yaml file in the root of your project. In the pubspec.yaml file, add an assets section and list all the assets you want to add. For example:

```
assets:
  - assets/icons/my_icon.png
  - assets/backgrounds/background.png
  - assets/fonts/Roboto.ttf
```

Once you have added the assets, run flutter pub get to download the packages and make them available to your application.

Conclusion

In conclusion, installing, creating and running a Flutter app is a straightforward process. With the right tools, such as Android Studio or Visual Studio Code, and the Flutter SDK, you can quickly get started on developing and testing your app. By following the steps outlined in this post, you can create a new project, run it on an emulator or real device, and experience the benefits of hot reload for fast, iterative development. With a solid foundation in place, you can continue to build and expand your Flutter app, taking advantage of the rich libraries and tools available in the Flutter ecosystem. Whether you're new to mobile development or an experienced developer, Flutter provides a fast, powerful and flexible platform for building beautiful and performant apps.

Multiple Choice Questions

1. **How do you create a new Flutter project?**
   a. Run the flutter create <project_name> command in the terminal.
   b. Use the File > New Project option in Android Studio or Visual Studio Code.
   c. Both A and B
2. **What is the main function in a Flutter application?**
   a. runApp()
   b. materialApp()
   c. startApp()
3. **What is the first screen that appears when you run the Flutter app?**
   a. The Login Screen
   b. The Home Screen
   c. The AppBar
4. **How do you open the emulator to run a Flutter app?**
   a. Use the flutter run command in the terminal.
   b. Use the Run > Run app option in Android Studio or Visual Studio Code.
   c. Both A and B
5. **What is hot reload in Flutter?**
   a. A feature that allows developers to see changes in the app in real-time
   b. A way to improve app performance
   c. A method for debugging code

6. **How can you test a Flutter app on a real device?**
    a. Use the flutter run command in the terminal.
    b. Connect your device to the computer and use the Run > Run app option in Android Studio or Visual Studio Code.
    c. Both A and B

7. **What is the difference between running a Flutter app on an emulator and a real device?**
    a. Emulators are faster than real devices.
    b. The appearance and performance may differ between an emulator and a real device.
    c. Emulators are easier to use than real devices.

Answers

1. **c**
2. **a**
3. **b**
4. **c**
5. **a**
6. **b**
7. **b**

CHAPTER 3

Widgets WidgetsWidgets!

Introduction

Welcome to the exciting world of Flutter widgets! Widgets are the building blocks of any Flutter app, and they are essential for creating engaging and interactive user interfaces. In this chapter, we will explore the most used widgets in Flutter and learn how to use them to build beautiful and responsive UIs. From basic widgets like Scaffold, Container and Text to more advanced ones like FutureBuilder and StreamBuilder, we'll cover them all.

We'll dive deep into the properties and attributes of each widget and learn how to customize them to fit our specific needs. We'll also explore how to combine widgets to create more complex and dynamic UI layouts.

By the end of this chapter, you'll have a solid understanding of the most important widgets in Flutter and be ready to start building your own beautiful and responsive apps. Let's get started and explore the exciting world of Flutter widgets!

Structure

In this chapter, we will cover the following topics:

- Understanding Widgets

- Basic Widgets
- Some more widgets

Understanding Widgets

Flutter is a powerful cross-platform framework that allows developers to create beautiful, fast, and responsive apps for both iOS and Android. At the heart of Flutter's user interface are widgets. In this blog post, we will explore what widgets are, how they work, and how to use them to create stunning UIs in your Flutter apps.

Widgets in Flutter are building blocks for creating user interfaces. These are the visual and functional elements of the app, such as buttons, text, images, and more. Widgets are what you see on the screen, and they are also responsible for how the app behaves.

In Flutter, everything is a widget, including the app itself. Every widget has a specific job to do, and you can combine multiple widgets to create complex UIs. Widgets can be arranged in a hierarchy, where each widget has a parent and zero or more children.

Widgets in Flutter have a simple life cycle. When you create a widget, it is immutable, meaning it cannot be changed. Instead, when you want to make a change to a widget, you create a new widget with the updated values.

When a widget is created, it goes through a process called layout. During this process, the widget determines its size and position on the screen. Once the layout is complete, the widget is painted on the screen.

Widgets can also have a state, which allows them to change over time. There are two types of states in Flutter: mutable and immutable. The mutable state can be changed, while the immutable state cannot. Widgets that have mutable states are called StatefulWidgets, while those with immutable states are called StatelessWidgets.

Using widgets in Flutter is easy. To create a new widget, simply extend the StatefulWidget or StatelessWidget class and implement the **`build()`** method. The **`build()`** method returns a widget that defines the UI of your app.

Now that you have a better understanding of widgets, let's get to know some popular widgets and how to use them.

Basic Widgets

Let's discuss some basic widgets.

Scaffold

Scaffold is a basic building block for creating the structure and layout of an app's user interface. It provides a pre-built set of commonly used UI components, such as an app bar, a floating action button, a drawer, and a bottom navigation bar. A Scaffold widget is usually the top-level widget in a Flutter app, and is used to provide a consistent visual and navigational structure across all the screens in the app.

Here is an example of how to use a Scaffold widget in a Flutter app:

```
class MyHomePage extends StatelessWidget {
  @override
  Widget build(BuildContext context) {
    return Scaffold(
      appBar: AppBar(
        title: Text('My App'),
      ),
      body: Center(
        child: Text('Hello, World!'),
      ),
      floatingActionButton: FloatingActionButton(
        onPressed: () {},
        child: Icon(Icons.add),
      ),
    );
  }
}
```

In this example, the Scaffold widget is used to create the basic structure of the app's home page. The app bar is defined using the appBar property, the main content of the page is defined using the body property, and the floating action button is defined using the floatingActionButton property. The body property is set to a Center widget that displays a simple text message.

The app bar displays a title (**My App**) using the Text widget, and it also includes a back button for navigating to the previous screen. The floating action button displays an icon (the add icon) and is used for triggering a specific action in the app.

By using the Scaffold widget, you can easily create a consistent user interface across all the screens in your Flutter app.

Container

Container is a widget that provides a rectangular visual element for holding other widgets. It is a flexible and customizable widget that can be used to add padding, borders, backgrounds, and other visual effects to its child widgets.

Here's an example of how to use a Container in the Flutter app.

```
class MainApp extends StatelessWidget {
  const MainApp({super.key});

  @override
  Widget build(BuildContext context) {
    return MaterialApp(
      home: Scaffold(
        body: Container(
          alignment: Alignment.center,
          padding: const EdgeInsets.all(16.0),
          margin: const EdgeInsets.symmetric(vertical: 8.0),
          decoration: BoxDecoration(
            color: Colors.blue,
            borderRadius: BorderRadius.circular(10.0),
            boxShadow: [
              BoxShadow(
                color: Colors.grey.withOpacity(0.5),
                spreadRadius: 5,
                blurRadius: 7,
                offset: const Offset(0, 3),
              ),
            ],
          ),
          child: const Text(
            'This is a Container widget',
            style: TextStyle(
              color: Colors.white,
```

```
              fontSize: 24.0,
            ),
          ),
        ),
      ),
    );
  }
}
```

In this example, the Container widget is used to display a text message with a blue background, rounded corners, and a shadow effect. The padding property adds space between the text and the edges of the container, while the margin property adds space between this container and other widgets around it. The decoration property sets up the visual effects of the container, including the color, border radius, and shadow. Finally, the child property sets the content of the container, which in this case is a Text widget.

Center

Center widget is used to horizontally and vertically center its child widget. It's a layout widget that takes one child and centers it within the available space.

Here's an example of how to use the Center widget in a Flutter app:

```
class MainApp extends StatelessWidget {
  const MainApp({super.key});

  @override
  Widget build(BuildContext context) {
    return const MaterialApp(
      home: Scaffold(
        body: Center(
          child: Text(
            'Hello, World!',
            style: TextStyle(fontSize: 24),
          ),
        ),
      ),
    );
  }
}
```

In this example, a Text widget with the label **Hello, World!** is centered horizontally and vertically using the Center widget. The text style is also set to use a font size of 24.

The Center widget is useful when you want to center a single widget within a parent widget. It can be used with any widget that has a fixed size or is able to determine its own size based on its contents. By using the Center widget, you can ensure that your app's UI is visually balanced and easy to read.

Text

Text widget is used to display a simple piece of text on the screen. It can be used to display anything from a single word to a complete paragraph. The Text widget provides a wide range of styling options, including font family, font size, font weight, text color, and text alignment.

Here is an example of how to use a Text widget in a Flutter app:

```
class MainApp extends StatelessWidget {
  const MainApp({super.key});

  @override
  Widget build(BuildContext context) {
    return const MaterialApp(
      home: Scaffold(
        body: Center(
          child: Text(
            'Hello, World!',
            style: TextStyle(
              fontSize: 24,
              fontWeight: FontWeight.bold,
              color: Colors.blue,
            ),
          ),
        ),
      ),
    );
  }
}
```

In this example, the Text widget is used to display the message "Hello, World!" in the center of the screen. The style property is used to customize the font size, font weight, and text color of the message.

By using the Text widget, you can easily display text on the screen in a Flutter app and customize its appearance to match your app's design.

Row

Row widget is used to display a horizontal row of child widgets. It lays out its children in a horizontal direction, either from left to right or from right to left, depending on the value of the textDirection property.

Here is an example of how to use a Row widget in a Flutter app:

```
class MainApp extends StatelessWidget {
  const MainApp({super.key});

  @override
  Widget build(BuildContext context) {
    return MaterialApp(
      home: Scaffold(
        body: Row(
          mainAxisAlignment: MainAxisAlignment.center,
          children: const [
            Text('Hello'),
            Text('World'),
          ],
        ),
      ),
    );
  }
}
```

In this example, the Row widget is used to display two text labels (“Hello” and "World") side by side in the center of the screen. The mainAxisAlignment property is used to specify how the children should be positioned horizontally within the row.

By using the Row widget, you can easily create a horizontal layout of child widgets in a Flutter app and customize the spacing and alignment of the children to match your app's design.

Column

Column widget is used to display a vertical column of child widgets. It lays out its children in a vertical direction, from top to bottom, with each child taking up as much space as it needs.

Here is an example of how to use a Column widget in a Flutter app:

```
class MainApp extends StatelessWidget {
  const MainApp({super.key});

  @override
  Widget build(BuildContext context) {
    return MaterialApp(
      home: Scaffold(
        body: Column(
          crossAxisAlignment: CrossAxisAlignment.start,
          children: const [
            Text(
              'Hello',
             style: TextStyle(fontSize: 24, fontWeight: FontWeight.bold),
            ),
            Text(
              'World',
             style: TextStyle(fontSize: 24, fontWeight: FontWeight.bold),
            ),
          ],
        ),
      ),
    );
  }
}
```

In this example, the Column widget is used to display the content of a book in a vertical layout, with each chapter being a separate child widget. CrossAxisAlignment property is used to specify how the children should be positioned horizontally within the column.

By using the Column widget, you can easily create a vertical layout of child widgets in a Flutter app and customize the spacing and alignment of the children to match your app's design. This makes it a useful widget for displaying textual content, such as books or articles.

SizedBox

SizedBox widget is used to create a box with a specified width and/or height. It is often used to create empty spaces between other widgets or to force widgets to be a certain size.

Here is an example of how to use a SizedBox widget in a Flutter app:

```
class MainApp extends StatelessWidget {
  const MainApp({super.key});

  @override
  Widget build(BuildContext context) {
    return MaterialApp(
      home: Scaffold(
        body: Column(
          mainAxisAlignment: MainAxisAlignment.center,
          children: [
            const Text(
              'This is some text.',
              style: TextStyle(fontSize: 24),
            ),
            const SizedBox(height: 20),
            const Text(
              'This is some more text.',
              style: TextStyle(fontSize: 24),
            ),
            const SizedBox(width: 50, height: 50),
            Container(
              width: 100,
              height: 100,
              color: Colors.blue,
            ),
          ],
        ),
      ),
    );
  }
}
```

In this example, a SizedBox widget is used to add some empty space between the two Text widgets. Another SizedBox widget is used to create a 50x50 box between the two Text widgets. Finally, a SizedBox widget is used to force the Container widget to have a width and height of 100.

By using the SizedBox widget, you can easily add empty spaces and force widgets to be a certain size in your Flutter app. This makes it a useful widget for achieving specific layout designs.

Stack

Stack widget is used to place one widget on top of another. It is useful for creating complex layouts where widgets need to overlap or be positioned in specific locations relative to each other.

Here's an example of how to use the Stack widget in a Flutter app:

```
class MainApp extends StatelessWidget {
  const MainApp({super.key});

  @override
  Widget build(BuildContext context) {
    return MaterialApp(
      home: Scaffold(
        body: Stack(
          children: [
            Container(
              width: 200,
              height: 200,
              color: Colors.blue,
            ),
            Positioned(
              top: 50,
              left: 50,
              child: Container(
                width: 100,
                height: 100,
                color: Colors.red,
              ),
            ),
            Positioned(
```

```
            bottom: 50,
            right: 50,
            child: Container(
              width: 100,
              height: 100,
              color: Colors.green,
            ),
          ),
        ],
      ),
    ),
  );
}
```

In this example, a Stack widget is used to place three Container widgets on top of each other. The first Container is blue and takes up the full size of the Stack. The second Container is positioned at the top left of the Stack and is red. The third Container is positioned at the bottom right of the Stack and is green.

Positioned widget is mainly used to place a child widget at a specific position relative to the top, right, bottom, or left of its parent widget.

By using the Stack widget and the Positioned widget, you can create complex layouts where widgets are positioned in specific locations relative to each other. This makes it a useful widget for creating custom designs and layouts in your Flutter app.

ElevatedButton

ElevatedButton widget is a Material Design style button that gives users the visual cue that it is a button that they can press. It has a raised appearance and responds to touches by changing its color.

Here's an example of how to use the ElevatedButton widget in a Flutter app:

```
class MainApp extends StatelessWidget {
  const MainApp({super.key});

  @override
  Widget build(BuildContext context) {
    return MaterialApp(
      home: Scaffold(
```

```
        body: Center(
          child: ElevatedButton(
            onPressed: () {
              print('Button clicked!');
            },
            child: const Text('Click me'),
          ),
        ),
      ),
    );
  }
}
```

In this example, an ElevatedButton widget is used to create a button with the label **`Click me`**. When the button is pressed, the onPressed callback is called and the message "Button clicked!" is printed to the console.

The ElevatedButton widget has several properties that can be used to customize its appearance and behavior, such as the button's color, text style, and disabled state. By using the ElevatedButton widget, you can quickly and easily create Material Design style buttons in your Flutter app.

Some more widgets

Some more Widgets are explained as follows.

Icons

Icon widget is used to display an icon in your app's UI. Icons are vector graphics that can be scaled to any size without losing their resolution or quality. Flutter provides a built-in library of icons that can be used out-of-the-box, or you can create your own custom icons.

Here's an example of how to use the Icon widget in a Flutter app:

```
class MainApp extends StatelessWidget {
  const MainApp({super.key});

  @override
  Widget build(BuildContext context) {
    return const MaterialApp(
      home: Scaffold(
```

```
        body: Center(
          child: Icon(
            Icons.favorite,
            color: Colors.red,
            size: 48,
          ),
        ),
      ),
    );
  }
}
```

In this example, an Icon widget is used to display a red heart icon with a size of 48 pixels. The Icon widget has three properties: the icon to display (in this case, Icons.favorite), the color of the icon, and the size of the icon.

Flutter provides a large library of built-in icons that you can use in your app. You can also create your own custom icons by creating vector graphics in a tool like Adobe Illustrator or Sketch and importing them into your Flutter project. By using the Icon widget, you can easily add icons to your app's UI and enhance its visual appeal.

Flexible

Flexible widget is used to create flexible layouts that can adapt to different screen sizes and orientations. The Flexible widget can be used to create rows and columns of widgets that can resize themselves based on the available space.

Here's an example of how to use the Flexible widget in a Flutter app:

```
class MainApp extends StatelessWidget {
  const MainApp({super.key});

  @override
  Widget build(BuildContext context) {
    return MaterialApp(
      home: Scaffold(
        body: Center(
          child: Row(
            children: [
              Flexible(
                flex: 1,
```

```
                child: Container(
                  color: Colors.blue,
                  height: 100,
                ),
              ),
              Flexible(
                flex: 2,
                child: Container(
                  color: Colors.green,
                  height: 100,
                ),
              ),
              Flexible(
                flex: 1,
                child: Container(
                  color: Colors.red,
                  height: 100,
                ),
              ),
            ],
          ),
        ),
      ),
    );
  }
}
```

In this example, a row of three containers is created using the Flexible widget. The first and third containers have a flex value of 1, while the second container has a flex value of 2. This means that the second container will take up twice as much space as the other two containers.

By using the Flexible widget, you can create dynamic and responsive layouts that can adjust to different screen sizes and orientations. This makes it easier to create apps that look great on all types of devices, from smartphones to tablets to desktops.

Expanded

Expanded widget is used to create flexible layouts that can adapt to different screen sizes and orientations. The Expanded widget can be used to create rows and columns of widgets that can resize themselves based on the available space.

Here's an example of how to use the Expanded widget in a Flutter app:

```
class MainApp extends StatelessWidget {
  const MainApp({super.key});
  @override
  Widget build(BuildContext context) {
    return MaterialApp(
      home: Scaffold(
        body: Column(
          children: [
            Expanded(
              flex: 1,
              child: Container(
                color: Colors.blue,
                height: 100,
              ),
            ),
            Expanded(
              flex: 2,
              child: Container(
                color: Colors.green,
                height: 100,
              ),
            ),
            Expanded(
              flex: 1,
              child: Container(
                color: Colors.red,
                height: 100,
              ),
            ),
          ],
        ),
      ),
    );
  }
}
```

In this example, a column of three containers is created using the Expanded widget. The first and third containers have a flex value of 1, while the second container has a flex value of 2. This means that the second container will take up twice as much space as the other two containers.

By using the Expanded widget, you can create dynamic and responsive layouts that can adjust to different screen sizes and orientations. This makes it easier to create apps that look great on all types of devices, from smartphones to tablets to desktops.

Image

Image widget is used to display images in the UI. You can use the Image widget to load images from a network, from the local file system, or from memory.

Here's an example of how to use the Image widget in a Flutter app:

```
class MainApp extends StatelessWidget {
  const MainApp({super.key});

  @override
  Widget build(BuildContext context) {
    return MaterialApp(
      home: Scaffold(
        body: Center(
          child: Image.network(
            'https://picsum.photos/250?image=9',
            width: 250,
            height: 250,
          ),
        ),
      ),
    );
  }
}
```

In this example, an image is loaded from the internet using the Image.network constructor. The image is displayed in the center of the screen using the Center widget. The width and height of the image are set to 250 pixels.

You can also use the Image.asset constructor to load images from the app's assets folder, or the Image.file constructor to load images from the local file system.

The Image widget provides a number of properties that you can use to customize the way the image is displayed, such as fit, alignment, and color. By using the Image widget, you can easily display images in your Flutter app and create rich and engaging user interfaces.

Form

Form widget is used to build forms in the UI. A form is a collection of user input controls such as text fields, checkboxes, and radio buttons. The Form widget provides a way to validate user input and submit the form data to a server or process it in some other way.

Here's an example of how to use the Form widget in a Flutter app:

```
class MainApp extends StatefulWidget {
  const MainApp({super.key});

  @override
  State<MainApp> createState() => _MainAppState();
}

class _MainAppState extends State<MainApp> {
  final _formKey = GlobalKey<FormState>();
  String? _name;
  String? _email;

  @override
  Widget build(BuildContext context) {
    return MaterialApp(
      home: Scaffold(
        body: Form(
          key: _formKey,
          child: Column(
            children: [
              TextFormField(
                decoration: const InputDecoration(labelText: 'Name'),
                validator: (String? value) {
                  if (value!.isEmpty) {
                    return 'Please enter your name';
                  }
```

```
                return null;
              },
              onSaved: (String? value) {
                _name = value;
              },
            ),
            TextFormField(
              decoration: const InputDecoration(labelText: 'Email'),
              validator: (String? value) {
                if (value!.isEmpty) {
                  return 'Please enter your email address';
                }
                return null;
              },
              onSaved: (String? value) {
                _email = value;
              },
            ),
            ElevatedButton(
              onPressed: () {
                if (_formKey.currentState!.validate()) {
                  _formKey.currentState!.save();
                  print('Name: $_name, Email: $_email');
                }
              },
              child: const Text('Submit'),
            ),
          ],
        ),
      ),
    ),
  );
 }
}
```

In this example, a simple form is created using the Form widget. The form contains two text input fields for the user's name and email address. The validator property of each text field is used to validate the user's input and display an error message if the input is invalid. The onSaved property is used to save the user's input into variables when the form is submitted.

The ElevatedButton widget is used to create a submit button. When the user taps the button, the **validate()** method is called on the FormState object, which checks that all the validators return null. If the validation succeeds, the onSaved callback is called for each field, and the form data is saved into the _name and _email variables. Finally, the form data is printed to the console.

By using the Form widget, you can easily create complex forms in your Flutter app with built-in validation and error handling.

FormField

FormField is a widget that provides the structure for a form field. It can be used to wrap input widgets such as text fields, dropdowns, checkboxes, and radio buttons to create a complete form.

FormField helps in validating user input and displaying error messages if the input is not valid. It can also track the state of the form field and notify the parent widget of any changes.

Here's an example of how to use FormField to create a text field with validation:

```
class MainApp extends StatefulWidget {
  const MainApp({super.key});

  @override
  State<MainApp> createState() => _MainAppState();
}

class _MainAppState extends State<MainApp> {
  final _formKey = GlobalKey<FormState>();
  String? _name;

  @override
  Widget build(BuildContext context) {
    return MaterialApp(
      home: Scaffold(
        body: Form(
          key: _formKey,
          child: Column(
            children: [
```

```
              TextFormField(
                decoration: const InputDecoration(
                  labelText: 'Name',
                ),
                validator: (String? value) {
                  if (value!.isEmpty) {
                    return 'Please enter your name';
                  }
                  return null;
                },
                onSaved: (value) {
                  _name = value;
                },
              ),
              ElevatedButton(
                onPressed: () {
                  if (_formKey.currentState!.validate()) {
                    _formKey.currentState!.save();
                    // Do something with the form data
                  }
                },
                child: const Text('Submit'),
              ),
            ],
          ),
        ),
      ),
    );
  }
}
```

In the preceding example, **TextFormField** is wrapped with FormField, and its validator property is set to check if the input is not empty. When the form is submitted, the validate method is called on the FormState, which in turn calls the validator on all its form fields. If the validation passes, the onSaved method is called, which updates the _name variable with the entered value.

The ElevatedButton is used to submit the form. When pressed, it calls the validate method on the form, which triggers the validation of all its form fields. If all the fields are valid, the onSaved method is called on each form field, and the form data can be used for further processing.

RichText

RichText widget in Flutter allows you to display formatted text with different styles, fonts, colors, and sizes. It is a powerful widget that enables you to create visually appealing text layouts for your app.

Here's an example of using the RichText widget to display text with different styles:

```
class MainApp extends StatelessWidget {
  const MainApp({super.key});

  @override
  Widget build(BuildContext context) {
    return MaterialApp(
      home: Scaffold(
        body: Center(
          child: RichText(
            text: const TextSpan(
              style: TextStyle(
                fontSize: 20.0,
                color: Colors.black,
              ),
              children: <TextSpan>[
                TextSpan(text: 'Flutter '),
                TextSpan(
                    text: 'is ', style: TextStyle(fontWeight:
                                                  FontWeight.bold)),
                TextSpan(text: 'awesome!'),
              ],
            ),
          ),
        ),
      ),
    );
  }
}
```

In this example, we are creating a RichText widget that displays the text "Flutter is awesome!" with the word "is" in bold. We achieve this by using the TextSpan widget, which is a child of the RichText widget. The TextSpan widget allows us to specify different styles for different parts of the text.

We start by defining the base style for the text using the style property of TextSpan. We then create three TextSpan children, one for each part of the text we want to style differently. The first TextSpan displays the word "Flutter" in the base style. The second TextSpan displays the word "is" in bold by setting the fontWeight property of the style to FontWeight.bold. The third TextSpan displays the word "awesome!" in the base style.

This is just a simple example of what you can do with the RichText widget. You can use it to create more complex text layouts with multiple styles and fonts.

Align

Align widget is used to align a child widget within its parent widget. It is similar to the positioning property in CSS, allowing you to place a widget in any position you want.

Here's an example of how to use the Align widget in Flutter:

```
class MainApp extends StatelessWidget {
  const MainApp({super.key});

  @override
  Widget build(BuildContext context) {
    return MaterialApp(
      home: Scaffold(
        body: Center(
          child: Container(
            height: 200,
            width: 200,
            color: Colors.grey,
            child: const Align(
              alignment: Alignment.bottomRight,
              child: FlutterLogo(
                size: 60,
              ),
            ),
          ),
```

```
        ),
      ),
    );
  }
}
```

In this example, we have a container widget with a grey background color and a height and width of 200 pixels. Within this container, we have an Align widget with a child FlutterLogo widget. The FlutterLogo widget is positioned in the bottom right corner of the container using the Alignment.bottomRight property of the Align widget.

You can use different values for the alignment property to position the child widget in different places within the parent widget. For example, Alignment. topLeft will position the child widget at the top left corner of the parent widget, and Alignment.center will position the child widget in the center of the parent widget.

The Align widget is useful when you need to position a child widget in a specific location within its parent widget.

ListView

ListView widget in Flutter is used to display a scrollable list of widgets that are too large to fit on the screen at once. It can be used to display a list of text, images, or any other widget that you want to scroll through.

Here's an example of how to use the ListView widget in Flutter:

```
class MainApp extends StatelessWidget {
  const MainApp({super.key});

  @override
  Widget build(BuildContext context) {
    return MaterialApp(
      home: Scaffold(
        body: Center(
          child: ListView(
            children: const [
              ListTile(
                leading: Icon(Icons.map),
                title: Text('Map'),
```

```
              ),
              ListTile(
                leading: Icon(Icons.photo_album),
                title: Text('Album'),
              ),
              ListTile(
                leading: Icon(Icons.phone),
                title: Text('Phone'),
              ),
            ],
          ),
        ),
      ),
    );
  }
}
```

In this example, we have a ListView widget with three children, each of which is a ListTile widget. The ListTile widget consists of an icon and a title, and it is used to display each item in the list. The ListView widget automatically creates a scrollable list of these items, and the user can scroll through the list to see all the items.

You can also use ListView.builder constructor to build a list of widgets dynamically based on the data you provide. This is useful when you have a large amount of data that needs to be displayed in a list, as it allows you to build only the items that are currently visible on the screen, instead of building all the items at once.

Overall, the ListView widget is a powerful tool for displaying large lists of widgets that can be scrolled through easily by the user. It is highly customizable and can be used to display a wide range of data in many different formats.

FutureBuilder

FutureBuilder widget in Flutter is a powerful tool that allows you to build widgets based on the results of a future. It is typically used when you need to fetch data asynchronously from an external source, such as a web API or a database, and then display that data in your app.

Here's an example of how to use the FutureBuilder widget in Flutter:

```
class MainApp extends StatelessWidget {
  const MainApp({super.key});

  @override
  Widget build(BuildContext context) {
    Future fetchUserData() async {
      await Future.delayed(const Duration(seconds: 2));
    }

    return MaterialApp(
      home: Scaffold(
        body: Center(
          child: FutureBuilder(
            future: fetchUserData(),
            builder: (context, snapshot) {
              if (snapshot.hasData) {
                // Build your widget based on the data returned by the
                                future
                return Text('Hello, ${snapshot.data['name']}!');
              } else if (snapshot.hasError) {
                // Handle any errors that occurred while fetching the
                                data
                return Text('Error: ${snapshot.error}');
              } else {
                // Show a loading indicator while the data is being
                                fetched
                return CircularProgressIndicator();
              }
            },
          ),
        ),
      ),
    );
  }
}
```

In this example, we have a FutureBuilder widget that is used to fetch user data asynchronously using the **fetchUserData()** function. The builder parameter of the FutureBuilder widget takes a callback function that is called with a snapshot object. The snapshot object contains information about the state of the future, including whether the future has been completed successfully or with an error, and whether it is still in progress.

If the snapshot object has data, we build a Text widget that displays a greeting message to the user using the data returned by the future. If the snapshot object has an error, we display an error message. If the future is still in progress, we display a loading indicator using the CircularProgressIndicator widget.

The FutureBuilder widget is a powerful tool for handling asynchronous data in Flutter, and it allows you to build dynamic and responsive UIs that update automatically as the data changes. It is a common pattern in Flutter apps that need to fetch data from external sources, and it can be customized in many ways to suit your specific use case.

StreamBuilder

StreamBuilder widget is used to build a widget tree that updates automatically whenever data is emitted from a stream. It is particularly useful when dealing with asynchronous data that arrives in the form of a stream.

Here's an example of how to use StreamBuilder in Flutter:

```
import 'dart:async';

class _MainAppState extends State<MainApp> {
  StreamController<int> _streamController = StreamController<int>();

  @override
  void dispose() {
    _streamController.close();
    super.dispose();
  }

  @override
  Widget build(BuildContext context) {
    return MaterialApp(
      home: Scaffold(
        body: Center(
          child: StreamBuilder<int>(
```

```
          stream: _streamController.stream,
          builder: (BuildContext context, AsyncSnapshot<int> snapshot) {
            if (snapshot.hasError) {
              Return const Text('Error: ${snapshot.error}');
            }
            if (!snapshot.hasData) {
              return Text('No data yet.');
            }
            return Text('Stream value: ${snapshot.data}');
          },
        ),
      ),
      floatingActionButton: FloatingActionButton(
        onPressed: () {
          _streamController.sink.add(DateTime.now().
                millisecondsSinceEpoch);
        },
        child: Icon(Icons.add),
      ),
    ),
  );
 }
}
```

In this example, we create a StreamController that emits an integer value whenever the FloatingActionButton is pressed. The StreamBuilder widget is then used to build the UI, with its stream property set to stream from the StreamController.

Whenever a new value is emitted from the stream, the builder function is called an AsyncSnapshot object containing the latest data. We can check the state of the snapshot (hasError, hasData, etc.) and return different UI widgets accordingly. In this example, we simply display the stream value in a Text widget when it's available.

The result is a widget that updates automatically as new data is emitted from the stream.

Conclusion

Widgets are the fundamental building blocks of any Flutter application. They allow developers to create a dynamic and responsive user interface with ease.

In this book, we covered various types of widgets, including basic widgets such as Text, Image, Icon, and Container, as well as more advanced widgets such as ListView, FutureBuilder, StreamBuilder, and more. You can find more widgets from Flutter's official documentation **https://docs.flutter.dev/development/ui/widgets**).

Each widget has its own purpose and functionality and mastering them can help you create powerful and efficient apps. Whether you're a beginner or an experienced developer, understanding widgets is essential for creating high-quality Flutter applications. We hope this book has provided you with a solid foundation for working with widgets and has sparked your curiosity to explore and experiment further. In the next chapter, we will learn about how to navigate and route your Flutter app.

Multiple Choice Questions

1. **Which widget is used to display a piece of text in a Flutter app?**
   a. Text
   b. Image
   c. Icon
   d. Container

2. **Which widget is used to display an image in a Flutter app?**
   a. Text
   b. Image
   c. Icon
   d. Container

3. **Which widget is used to display an icon in the Flutter app?**
   a. Text
   b. Image
   c. Icon
   d. Container

4. **Which widget is used to group other widgets together in a row, allowing them to be displayed horizontally?**
   a. Text
   b. Image

   c. Icon
   d. Row

5. **Which widget is used to group other widgets together in a column, allowing them to be displayed vertically?**
   a. Text
   b. Image
   c. Icon
   d. Column

6. **Which widget is used to create a button in a Flutter app?**
   a. ElevatedButton
   b. FlatButton
   c. IconButton
   d. RaiscdButton

7. **Which widget is used to create a container in a Flutter app that can be used to group other widgets and apply padding or margins?**
   a. Text
   b. Image
   c. Icon
   d. Container

8. **Which widget is used to create a scrollable list of items in a Flutter app?**
   a. Text
   b. Image
   c. Icon
   d. ListView

Answers

1. **a**
2. **b**
3. **c**

4. **d**
5. **d**
6. **a**
7. **d**
8. **d**

References

https://docs.flutter.dev/development/ui/widgets

CHAPTER 4

Stateful and Stateless Widgets

Introduction

Stateful and stateless widgets are the core building blocks of any Flutter application. These widgets are used to build dynamic UI elements that can respond to user interaction and data changes in real-time. In this chapter, we will explore the differences between stateful and stateless widgets and learn how to use them effectively in your Flutter applications.

Understanding the difference between stateful and stateless widgets is crucial to building performant and efficient Flutter applications. In this chapter, we will learn how to use stateful and stateless widgets to build dynamic and responsive UI elements. We will explore different techniques for managing state in Flutter, including using the **`setState()`** method, InheritedWidgets, and Provider package.

Throughout the chapter, we will use practical examples to illustrate the concepts and techniques discussed. By the end of this chapter, you will have a thorough understanding of stateful and stateless widgets and how to use them effectively in your Flutter applications. You will also learn best practices for managing state in Flutter and be able to build complex, responsive UI elements that can handle user interaction and data changes in real-time.

Structure

In this chapter, we will cover the following topics:

- Introduction to Stateless and Stateful widgets
- Choosing between Stateless and Stateful widgets
- Using Stateless widget
- Using Stateful widget

Introduction to Stateless and Stateful Widgets

This section is exploring on StatelessWidgets and StatefulWidgets.

StatelessWidget

StatelessWidget is a fundamental concept used to build user interface elements that do not change their state during their lifetime. It represents a widget that is immutable, meaning its properties and appearance cannot change once it is created. StatelessWidget is an essential building block in Flutter app development and is widely used to create various UI components.

Key features of StatelessWidget

- **Immutable Widget:** StatelessWidget is immutable, meaning it cannot change its properties or appearance once it is created. This ensures a consistent user interface and reduces the risk of unexpected side effects.
- **Fast and Lightweight:** Since StatelessWidget does not need to handle state changes, it is fast and lightweight, resulting in better performance and a smoother user experience.
- **Ideal for Static UI:** StatelessWidget is perfect for building UI components that do not require updates or dynamic changes based on user interactions.
- **Stateless Hot Reload:** When using StatelessWidget, Flutter's hot reload feature is even more efficient because the widget does not have any mutable state.

Benefits of Using StatelessWidget

- **Performance Optimization:** By using StatelessWidget for static UI components, the app's performance improves, resulting in faster rendering and smoother animations.
- **Code Simplicity:** StatelessWidget reduces the complexity of managing state, simplifying the codebase and making it easier to maintain and debug.
- **Hot Reload Efficiency:** StatelessWidget makes the hot reload process faster and more reliable, allowing developers to iterate and experiment with the UI quickly.

StatefulWidget

StatefulWidget is a fundamental concept used to build user interface elements that can change their state during their lifetime. It represents a widget that is mutable, allowing it to update its properties and appearance dynamically based on user interactions or external data changes. StatefulWidget is a powerful tool in Flutter app development, enabling developers to create interactive and dynamic user interfaces.

Key features of StatefulWidget

- **Mutable Widget:** StatefulWidget is mutable, meaning it can change its state over time. This allows the widget to respond to user interactions or update its content based on external data changes.
- **Reactive UI Updates:** When the state of a StatefulWidget changes, Flutter triggers a rebuild of the widget, ensuring that the UI reflects the latest state accurately.
- **Ideal for Dynamic UI:** StatefulWidget is perfect for building UI components that require updates and dynamic changes based on user interactions, data fetch, or other events.
- **Stateful Hot Reload:** Flutter's hot reload feature works seamlessly with StatefulWidget, enabling developers to see real-time changes to the widget state during development.

Benefits of Using StatefulWidget

- **Interactivity and Responsiveness:** By using StatefulWidget, developers can create responsive user interfaces that react to user input, data changes, and other events in real-time.

- **Dynamic Content:** StatefulWidget enables the creation of UI components that can change their appearance, content, or behavior based on dynamic data sources, providing a more personalized user experience.
- **Efficient State Management:** StatefulWidget incorporates efficient state management, allowing developers to handle complex state changes while keeping the code organized and maintainable.

Choosing between Stateless and Stateful Widgets

So, how do you choose between the two? Here are some tips to help you decide:

- **Consider the widget's purpose:** If the widget's appearance is fixed and won't change, then use a stateless widget. If the widget's appearance or content can change based on user input or other events, then use a stateful widget.
- **Think about performance:** Stateless widgets are faster and use less memory than stateful widgets because they don't need to manage any state. If performance is a concern, then try to use stateless widgets whenever possible.
- **Keep it simple:** If your widget doesn't need to change, then don't make it stateful just for the sake of it. Keeping it stateless will make your code simpler and easier to maintain. *Table 4.1* shows the differences between Stateless and Stateful Widgets.

Stateless Widgets	Stateful Widgets
When you need to display static information, like text or images	When you need to handle user interactions, like button presses or form submissions
When you need to display data that does not change frequently	When you need to manage data that changes frequently, like user input or network requests
When you need to build simple widgets with minimal code	When you need to build more complex widgets with custom behavior or animations

***Table 4.1**: Difference between Stateless and Stateful Widgets*

In conclusion, understanding the difference between stateless and stateful widgets is important for building efficient and performant Flutter apps. Consider the purpose of your widget and the performance implications before deciding which type of widget to use.

Using Stateless Widget

To use a Stateless widget in Flutter, you first need to create a new widget class that extends the `StatelessWidget` base class. The widget class needs to override the build method, which returns the widget tree that the widget should render.

Let's take an example of a simple text widget that displays a greeting message. Here's the code for the widget:

```
import 'package:flutter/material.dart';


class GreetingWidget extends StatelessWidget {
  @override
  Widget build(BuildContext context) {
    return Text(
      'Hello, Flutter!',
      style: TextStyle(fontSize: 24),
    );
  }
}
```

In this example, we've created a new widget class called `GreetingWidget` that extends the `StatelessWidget` class. The build method returns a `Text` widget that displays the greeting message.

To use this widget in your Flutter app, you can simply add it to the widget tree of another widget, like this:

```
import 'package:flutter/material.dart';


class HomePage extends StatelessWidget {
  @override
  Widget build(BuildContext context) {
    return Scaffold(
      appBar: AppBar(
        title: Text('My App'),
      ),
      body: Center(
        child: GreetingWidget(),
```

```
      ),
    );
  }
}
```

In this example, we're using the `GreetingWidget` as a child of the `Center` widget. The `Center` widget aligns its child in the center of the screen. The `GreetingWidget` is a `Stateless widget`, so it doesn't need to maintain any state.

Overall, using stateless widgets in Flutter is a straightforward process. It's essential to understand the difference between stateless and stateful widgets and when to use them. Stateless widgets are useful for creating simple UI components that don't require any mutable state.

Using Stateful Widget

Creating a stateful widget in Flutter involves two main steps:

1. Create a stateful widget class that extends StatefulWidget.
2. Create a state class that extends State and manages the mutable state for the widget.

Let's create a simple example of a stateful widget in Flutter. We will create a counter app that displays a button and a counter. Each time the button is pressed, the counter will increment.

Step 1: Create the `StatefulWidget` class.

```
class CounterApp extends StatefulWidget {
  @override
  _CounterAppState createState() => _CounterAppState();
}
```

In this code, we define a new class called `CounterApp` that extends `StatefulWidget`. We also override the `createState` method to return an instance of `_CounterAppState`.

Step 2: Create the `State` class.

```
class _CounterAppState extends State<CounterApp> {
  int _counter = 0;

  void _incrementCounter() {
    setState(() {
      _counter++;
```

```
    });
  }

  @override
  Widget build(BuildContext context) {
    return Scaffold(
      appBar: AppBar(
        title: Text('Counter App'),
      ),
      body: Center(
        child: Column(
          mainAxisAlignment: MainAxisAlignment.center,
          children: <Widget>[
            Text(
              'Counter Value:',
            ),
            Text(
              '$_counter',
              style: Theme.of(context).textTheme.headline4,
            ),
          ],
        ),
      ),
      floatingActionButton: FloatingActionButton(
        onPressed: _incrementCounter,
        tooltip: 'Increment',
        child: Icon(Icons.add),
      ),
    );
  }
}
```

In this code, we define a new class called `_CounterAppState` that extends `State`. We also define an integer `_counter` that will be used to store the current counter value. The `_incrementCounter` method is called each time the button is pressed and uses the `setState` method to update the `_counter value`.

The build method returns a `Scaffold` widget that contains a `Column` widget with two `Text` widgets and a `FloatingActionButton`. The first `Text` widget displays a static message, while the second `Text` widget displays the current value of the `_counter` variable.

Tip: You can create a Stateless or Stateful Widget easily in VS Code with the help of Flutter extension. Create a .dart file and type stl (*Figure* 4.1).

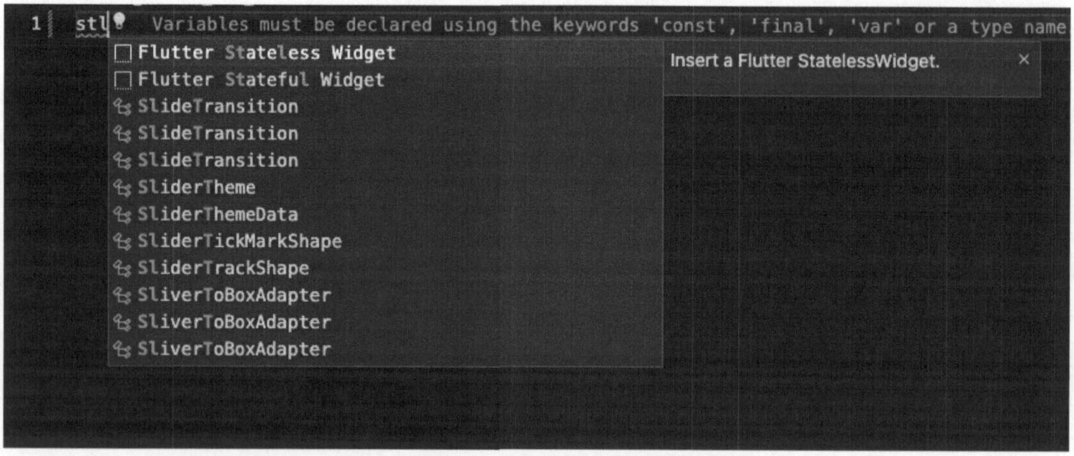

***Figure* 4.1**: *VS Code Flutter Extension*

Stateful Widget Lifecycle: initState, didUpdateWidget, and more

StatefulWidget has a rich lifecycle that allows developers to manage and react to changes in the widget's state. Understanding the various lifecycle methods of a StatefulWidget is essential for handling state changes, performing initialization, and managing resources efficiently.

1. **initState()**
   - The **`initState()`** method is called when the StatefulWidget is inserted into the widget tree for the first time.
   - It is used to perform one-time initialization tasks, such as setting up listeners, initializing variables, or fetching initial data from a database or API.
   - This method is called before the **`build()`** method is executed.

```
class MyStatefulWidget extends StatefulWidget {
  @override
  _MyStatefulWidgetState createState() => _
MyStatefulWidgetState();
```

```
}

class _MyStatefulWidgetState extends State<MyStatefulWidget> {
  @override
  void initState() {
    super.initState();
    // Perform one-time initialization tasks here.
    fetchDataFromServer();
  }

  void fetchDataFromServer() {
    // Fetch initial data from a server.
  }

  @override
  Widget build(BuildContext context) {
    // Widget build implementation.
  }
}
```

2. **didChangeDependencies()**

- The **`didChangeDependencies()`** method is called when the StatefulWidget's dependencies (e.g., inherited widgets) change.
- It is useful for reacting to changes in inherited widget data and updating the widget accordingly.

```
class MyStatefulWidget extends StatefulWidget {
  @override
  _MyStatefulWidgetState createState() => _
MyStatefulWidgetState();
}

class _MyStatefulWidgetState extends State<MyStatefulWidget> {
  @override
  void didChangeDependencies() {
    super.didChangeDependencies();
    // React to changes in inherited widget data here.
  }
```

```
  @override
  Widget build(BuildContext context) {
    // Widget build implementation.
  }
}
```

3. **didUpdateWidget()**

- The **`didUpdateWidget()`** method is called whenever the StatefulWidget is rebuilt with new configuration.
- It allows you to compare the old and new widget instances and respond to changes, such as updating the state or performing additional tasks.

```
class MyStatefulWidget extends StatefulWidget {
  final int value;

  MyStatefulWidget({required this.value});

  @override
  _MyStatefulWidgetState createState() => _
MyStatefulWidgetState();
}

class _MyStatefulWidgetState extends State<MyStatefulWidget> {
  int previousValue = 0;

  @override
  void didUpdateWidget(MyStatefulWidget oldWidget) {
    super.didUpdateWidget(oldWidget);
    if (widget.value != previousValue) {
      // React to changes in the 'value' property.
      previousValue = widget.value;
    }
  }

  @override
  Widget build(BuildContext context) {
    // Widget build implementation.
  }
}
```

4. **dispose()**

- The **`dispose()`** method is called when the StatefulWidget is removed from the widget tree.
- It is used to clean up resources, such as canceling subscriptions, closing streams, or disposing of controllers.
- Always remember to release resources in this method to avoid memory leaks.

```
class MyStatefulWidget extends StatefulWidget {
  @override
  _MyStatefulWidgetState createState() => _
MyStatefulWidgetState();
}

class _MyStatefulWidgetState extends State<MyStatefulWidget> {
  StreamSubscription _streamSubscription;

  @override
  void initState() {
    super.initState();
    _streamSubscription = someStream.listen((data) {
      // Handle incoming data from the stream.
    });
  }

  @override
  void dispose() {
    _streamSubscription.cancel();
    super.dispose();
  }

  @override
  Widget build(BuildContext context) {
    // Widget build implementation.
  }
}
```

Managing State: Using setState() and InheritedWidget

Managing state is a critical aspect of building dynamic and interactive user interfaces. Two common methods for managing state in a StatefulWidget are **`setState()`** and InheritedWidget. Both approaches offer unique solutions to handle state changes, depending on the complexity and scope of the state management requirements.

Using setState() for Local State Management

`setState()` is a method provided by the StatefulWidget class, allowing developers to manage changes to the widget's state within its associated State class. It is particularly useful for handling simple state changes that are local to a specific widget.

How setState() works

- When **`setState()`** is called, Flutter schedules a rebuild of the widget and its subtree, updating the UI to reflect the new state.
- The **`build()`** method is re-executed with the updated state, and the changes are efficiently rendered on the screen.

```
class CounterWidget extends StatefulWidget {
  @override
  _CounterWidgetState createState() => _CounterWidgetState();
}

class _CounterWidgetState extends State<CounterWidget> {
  int _counter = 0;

  void _incrementCounter() {
    setState(() {
      _counter++;
    });
  }

  @override
  Widget build(BuildContext context) {
    return Column(
      children: [
```

```
          Text('Counter: $_counter'),
          ElevatedButton(
            onPressed: _incrementCounter,
            child: Text('Increment'),
          ),
        ],
      );
    }
  }
```

In this example, when the **Increment** button is pressed, the _counter state is updated using **setState()**. As a result, the **build()** method is called again with the updated state, and the new value of _counter is displayed on the screen.

Using InheritedWidget for Global State Management

InheritedWidget is a powerful mechanism for managing state across multiple widgets in the widget tree. It allows passing data down the widget tree without explicitly passing it through each widget's constructor.

How InheritedWidget works

- A data-holding InheritedWidget is created to hold the shared state data.
- Widgets can access this shared data using the InheritedWidget's of() method, which returns the closest instance of the widget found in the widget tree.
- When the shared state changes, the **InheritedWidget** notifies its dependents, triggering a rebuild of widgets that depend on the shared data.

```
class AppState extends InheritedWidget {
  final int counter;

  AppState({Key key, this.counter, Widget child}) : super(key: key, child: child);

  @override
  bool updateShouldNotify(covariant AppState oldWidget) {
    return counter != oldWidget.counter;
  }
```

```
  static AppState of(BuildContext context) {
    return context.
dependOnInheritedWidgetOfExactType<AppState>();
  }
}

class CounterWidget extends StatelessWidget {
  @override
  Widget build(BuildContext context) {
    final appState = AppState.of(context);

    return Column(
      children: [
        Text('Counter: ${appState.counter}'),
        ElevatedButton(
          onPressed: () {
            // Increment the counter in the shared state.
            appState.counter++;
          },
          child: Text('Increment'),
        ),
      ],
    );
  }
}
```

In this example, we create an AppState class that extends InheritedWidget to hold the shared state data, counter. The CounterWidget can access this shared data using the **`AppState.of(context)`** method, and when the **`Increment`** button is pressed, the shared counter state is updated. As a result, all widgets depending on the AppState will be rebuilt to reflect the updated state.

Managing state is a crucial aspect of Flutter app development, and the choice between **`setState()`** and InheritedWidget depends on the scope and complexity of state management. For local state changes within a single widget, **`setState()`** works efficiently, while InheritedWidget is recommended for managing shared state across the widget tree. By understanding and utilizing these state management approaches effectively, developers can build robust and responsive Flutter applications.

Conclusion

Both stateless and stateful widgets have their own unique features and can be used in various scenarios depending on the requirements of the application. Stateless widgets are useful for displaying UI elements that don't require dynamic data or user interactions. They are lightweight and fast, making them ideal for widgets that don't change frequently.

On the other hand, stateful widgets are used when the UI needs to change dynamically in response to user input or other external factors. They store data and have a built-in mechanism for updating the UI in response to changes in that data.

Choosing between these two widget types depends on the specific needs of the application. It's important to consider the performance implications and complexity of the widget hierarchy when deciding which type to use.

Regardless of which widget type you choose, it's important to follow best practices for structuring your code and managing state to ensure that your application is maintainable and scalable over time.

In the next chapter, we will delve deeper into the concept of navigation and routing in Flutter. Navigation is a critical aspect of mobile app development, as it enables users to move between different screens or pages seamlessly. Flutter provides a powerful set of navigation tools, including named routes, route generation functions, and page transitions. We will explore how to use these features to build smooth and intuitive navigation experiences for our users. Additionally, we will cover advanced topics such as deep linking, navigation stacks, and route management. With this knowledge, you will be able to create polished and sophisticated navigation flows in your Flutter apps.

Task

From this chapter onwards you'll be getting a small task based on what we learned from each chapter. We encourage you to take your time with this activity and experiment with different approaches to solve the problem. Don't worry if you get stuck or make mistakes - that's all part of the learning process! In case you could not get through we you can access our GitHub repository (**https://github.com/lahirunc/task_tracker**) and get the solution.

Once you have completed the activity, take some time to reflect on your journey with Flutter and how far you have come. So, let's start building our first Flutter app!

1. Open VS Code and create a new flutter project named `task_tracker`.
2. Create a folder named `screens` inside the `lib` folder.
3. Inside the `screens` folder create two files, `home_screen.dart` and `create_task_screen.dart`.
4. In the `home_screen.dart` file, create a new Stateless widget called `HomeScreen`. This widget will be the home screen of your app.
5. In the `HomeScreen` widget, add a Scaffold widget as the top-level widget. Inside the Scaffold, add an AppBar with the title `Task Tracker` and body `Container`.
6. Now add a `FloatingActionButton` inside the Scaffold after the body, and inside the `FloatingActionButton`, add `child` and `onPressed` as shown below.

```
floatingActionButton: FloatingActionButton(
        onPressed: () {},
        child: const Icon(Icons.add),
      ),
```

7. Now go back to the `main.dart` file and delete all the comments. Then delete title: 'Flutter Demo', inside the `MaterialApp`.

You can easily delete all the comments in the `main.dart` file in VS Code by using the find and replace tool. Simply press `Ctrl+F`, type in the regular expression `//.*`, select the regex option in the find tool, and then replace it with an empty string. This will remove all single-line comments in the file, making it easier to read and navigate.

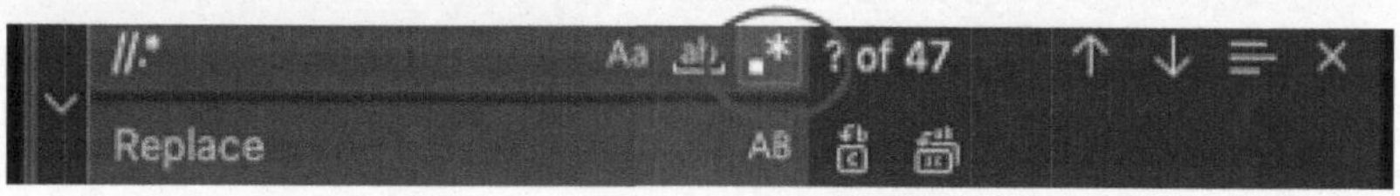

Figure 4.2: *VS Code Flutter Find & Replace*

8. Next, delete the `MyHomePage StatefulWidget` and finally, replace the home tag with `const HomeScreen()`.

```
home: const HomeScreen(),
```

9. Go to `create_task_screen.dart` and create a `StatefulWidget` and return a `Center. Inside the Center widget add a Text('Create Task')`.

Questions

1. **What is the main difference between a Stateless and a Stateful widget in Flutter?**
    a. A stateless widget has no state, while a stateful widget can change its state.
    b. A Stateless widget has a mutable state, while a Stateful widget has an immutable state.
    c. A Stateless widget can only be used once, while a Stateful widget can be used multiple times.
    d. There is no difference between a Stateless and a Stateful widget.

2. **When should you use a stateless widget in Flutter?**
    a. When you need to change the widget's state over time.
    b. When the widget's content depends on its parent widget's state.
    c. When the widget's content never changes.
    d. When you need to make a network request.

3. **When should you use a Stateful widget in Flutter?**
    a. When the widget's content never changes.
    b. When the widget's content depends on its parent widget's state.
    c. When you need to make network requests.
    d. When you need to animate the widget.

4. **Which method is used to build the UI for a stateful widget in Flutter?**
    a. build()
    b. initState()
    c. dispose()
    d. None of the above

5. **What is the purpose of the "initState" method in a Stateful widget in Flutter?**
    a. To create the widget's initial state.
    b. To update the widget's state whenever it changes.
    c. To dispose of the widget when it is no longer needed.
    d. To handle user input.

6. **What is the main advantage of using a stateful widget in Flutter?**
    a. They are faster than stateless widgets.
    b. They can have interaction with the user.
    c. They can change their internal state.
    d. They have a simpler implementation.

Answers

1. **a**
2. **b**
3. **b**
4. **a**
5. **a**
6. **c**

References

- **https://docs.flutter.dev/development/ui/interactive**

Chapter 5
Navigation and Routing

Introduction

Welcome to the exciting world of Flutter navigation and routing! Navigation and routing are essential parts of any mobile app, and Flutter provides a powerful and flexible navigation system that allows developers to create complex navigation flows with ease. In this chapter, we will explore the different navigation and routing techniques available in Flutter and will learn how to use them to create intuitive and user-friendly mobile apps.

We'll start by exploring the basics of navigation and routing in Flutter, including how to navigate between different screens in your app using buttons and other UI elements. We'll then dive deeper into the more advanced navigation and routing concepts, such as named routes and modal dialogs.

We'll also cover topics like passing data between screens, customizing the appearance of navigation elements, and implementing animations and transitions to enhance the user experience.

By the end of this chapter, you'll have a solid understanding of navigation and routing in Flutter and be ready to start building your own intuitive and user-friendly mobile apps. So, let's dive in and explore the exciting world of Flutter navigation and routing!

Structure

In this chapter, we will cover the following topics:

- Introduction to Navigator
- Working of the Navigator
- Using Navigator to route
- Model Dialogs

Introduction to Navigator

The Navigator widget is an essential component in Flutter that manages the navigation stack and enables smooth screen transitions within an app. It serves as a navigator for the user, allowing them to move between different screens or pages effortlessly. Understanding the Navigator widget is crucial for implementing effective navigation in Flutter applications.

In Flutter, the Navigator widget is responsible for maintaining a stack of routes. Each route represents a screen or page in the app. When the user navigates to a new screen, the Navigator pushes the corresponding route onto the stack. Similarly, when the user goes back, the topmost route is popped from the stack.

To interact with the Navigator, you need to access the current context. The context provides access to the Navigator and allows you to perform navigation operations such as pushing, popping, and replacing routes. By leveraging the Navigator widget, you can create a structured and intuitive navigation flow for your app.

Working of the Navigator

When building a mobile app in Flutter, it is important to have a robust and flexible navigation system. This is where the Navigator comes into play. The Navigator is a widget in Flutter that manages a stack of routes and provides an intuitive way to navigate between screens. But how exactly does the Navigator work?

At its core, the Navigator maintains a stack of Route objects. A Route represents a screen or page in the app and can be either a full-screen or dialog-style window. When the user navigates to a new screen, a new Route is pushed onto the stack, and when the user navigates back, the top Route is popped off the stack.

The Navigator widget provides several methods for manipulating the Route stack. For example, the **`push()`** method is used to add a new Route to the stack, while the **`pop()`** method is used to remove the top Route. Additionally, the

Navigator provides support for transitions between Routes, such as sliding or fading animations.

One important thing to note about the Navigator is that it is hierarchical. This means that you can have nested Navigators within your app, each managing its own stack of Routes.

Overall, the Navigator is a powerful and essential tool for building complex mobile apps in Flutter. With its intuitive navigation stack and support for transitions, it provides a seamless user experience that can help take your app to the next level.

Using Navigator to route

Navigating to a New Route

To navigate to a new route, you can use the **Navigator.push()** method. This method takes a **BuildContext** object and a MaterialPageRoute object that specifies the new route to display. The new route is then added to the top of the navigation stack.

```
class HomeScreen extends StatelessWidget {
  @override
  Widget build(BuildContext context) {
    return Scaffold(
      appBar: AppBar(
        title: Text('Home Screen'),
      ),
      body: Center(
        child: ElevatedButton(
          child: Text('Go to Details'),
          onPressed: () {
            Navigator.push(
              context,
              MaterialPageRoute(builder: (context) => DetailsScreen()),
            );
          },
        ),
      ),
    );
  }
}
```

In the preceding code, we have added an ElevatedButton to the home screen that navigates to the details screen when pressed. When the button is pressed, the **Navigator.push()** method is called, passing the context object and the DetailsScreen object as arguments.

Passing Data to a New Route

You can pass data to a new route by specifying it in the constructor of the new route's widget. In the following example, we have added a constructor to the DetailsScreen widget that takes a String parameter named 'itemId'. This parameter is used to display the details of the selected item.

```
class DetailsScreen extends StatelessWidget {
  final String itemId;

  DetailsScreen({@required this.itemId});

  @override
  Widget build(BuildContext context) {
    return Scaffold(
      appBar: AppBar(
        title: Text('Details Screen'),
      ),
      body: Center(
        child: Text('Item $itemId'),
      ),
    );
  }
}
```

To pass data to the new route, you can add it to the **MaterialPageRoute** object's constructor. In the following code, we have added the itemId data to the DetailsScreen constructor.

```
Navigator.push(
  context,
  MaterialPageRoute(builder: (context) => DetailsScreen(itemId: '1')),
);
```

Navigating Back

To navigate back to the previous route, you can use the **Navigator.pop()** method. This method removes the current route from the navigation stack and displays the previous route.

```
class DetailsScreen extends StatelessWidget {
  final String itemId;

  DetailsScreen({@required this.itemId});

  @override
  Widget build(BuildContext context) {
    return Scaffold(
      appBar: AppBar(
        title: Text('Details Screen'),
      ),
      body: Center(
        child: RaisedButton(
          child: Text('Go Back'),
          onPressed: () {
            Navigator.pop(context);
          },
        ),
      ),
    );
  }
}
``
```

Using Named route

Adding Named Routes

To use named routes with the Flutter Navigator, you must first add them to your application. You can do this by defining a Map of named routes in your MaterialApp widget's routes parameter. The key to each entry is the route name, and the value is a function that returns the widget for that route.

```
class MyApp extends StatelessWidget {
  @override
  Widget build(BuildContext context) {
    return MaterialApp(
      initialRoute: '/',
      routes: {
        '/': (context) => HomeScreen(),
```

```
        '/details': (context) => DetailsScreen(),
      },
    );
  }
}
```

In the preceding code, we have added two named routes: the home route and the details route. The home route is the default route, and it is displayed when the application is launched. The details route is used to display additional information about an item on the home screen.

Navigating to a Named Route

To navigate to a named route, you can use the **`Navigator.pushNamed()`** method. This method takes a context object and the name of the route to navigate to as arguments. The new route is then added to the top of the navigation stack.

```
class HomeScreen extends StatelessWidget {
  @override
  Widget build(BuildContext context) {
    return Scaffold(
      appBar: AppBar(
        title: Text('Home Screen'),
      ),
      body: Center(
        child: ElevatedButton(
          child: Text('Go to Details'),
          onPressed: () {
            Navigator.pushNamed(context, '/details');
          },
        ),
      ),
    );
  }
}
```

In the preceding code, we have added an ElevatedButton to the home screen that navigates to the details screen when pressed. When the button is pressed, the Navigator.pushNamed() method is called, passing the context object and the name of the details route as arguments.

Passing Data to a Named Route

You can pass data to a named route by specifying it in the route's arguments parameter. In the following example, we have added an arguments parameter to the DetailsScreen route that takes a String parameter named 'itemId'. This parameter is used to display the details of the selected item.

```
class DetailsScreen extends StatelessWidget {
  static const routeName = '/details';

  @override
  Widget build(BuildContext context) {
    final itemId = ModalRoute.of(context).settings.arguments as String;

    return Scaffold(
      appBar: AppBar(
        title: Text('Details Screen'),
      ),
      body: Center(
        child: Text('Item $itemId'),
      ),
    );
  }
}
```

To pass data to the new route, you can add it to the Navigator.pushNamed() method's arguments parameter. In the following code, we have added the itemId data to the details route's arguments.

```
Navigator.pushNamed(
  context,
  DetailsScreen.routeName,
  arguments: '1',
);
```

Navigating Back

To navigate back to the previous route, you can use the Navigator.pop() method. This method removes the current route from the navigation stack and displays the previous route.

```
class DetailsScreen extends StatelessWidget {
  @override
```

```
  Widget build(BuildContext context) {
    return Scaffold(
      appBar: AppBar(
        title: Text('Details Screen'),
      ),
      body: Center(
        child: ElevatedButton(
          child: Text('Go Back'),
          onPressed: () {
            Navigator.pop(context);
          },
        ),
      ),
    );
  }
}
```

In the preceding code, we have added an ElevatedButton to the details screen that navigates back to the home screen when pressed. When the button is pressed, the Navigator.pop() method is called, passing the context object as an argument.

Note: In this book, we will be using Navigator to navigate.

Model Dialogs

Model dialogs are an essential part of mobile applications. They help the user to make informed decisions by displaying important information or asking for confirmation before executing a particular action. In this blog post, we will explore how to create model dialogs in Flutter and provide some examples of their usage.

A model dialog is a pop-up window that displays important information or requests user input before proceeding with a particular action. It appears on top of the current screen and requires user interaction to dismiss it. In Flutter, the Model Dialog class is provided by the **showDialog** function.

Creating a model dialog in Flutter is straightforward. The **showDialog** function is used to create a pop-up window that displays content or prompts user input. The **showDialog** function takes in a **BuildContext** object and a **builder** method. The **builder** method is used to build the content of the dialog window. Here is an example of how to create a model dialog:

```
showDialog(
  context: context,
  builder: (BuildContext context) {
    return AlertDialog(
      title: Text("Dialog Title"),
      content: Text("Dialog content goes here."),
      actions: [
        TextButton(
          child: Text("Cancel"),
          onPressed: () {
            Navigator.of(context).pop();
          },
        ),
        ElevatedButton(
          child: Text("OK"),
          onPressed: () {
            // Perform action
            Navigator.of(context).pop();
          },
        ),
      ],
    );
  },
);
```

In the above example, we create a model dialog with a title, content, and two buttons, **`Cancel`** and **`OK`**. The **`ElevatedButton`** widgets are used to handle the button's actions. The **`Navigator.of(context).pop()`** method is used to dismiss the dialog.

Dialog Types Model

Flutter provides different types of model dialogs that can be used to display different types of content. Here are some of the most common ones:

Simple Dialog

Simple Dialogs in Flutter are an important element that allows developers to display small, context-specific overlays on top of the current screen. They provide a non-intrusive way to interact with users, presenting a set of options or actions without navigating away from the current context. Simple dialogs are lightweight, easy to implement, and serve as a user-friendly means to make selections or seek user input without disrupting the user's current workflow.

In this section, we will explore the basics of Simple Dialogs in Flutter and how to create one using the built-in **showDialog()** method along with the SimpleDialog widget.

Example of a Simple Dialog in Flutter:

```
void _showSimpleDialog(BuildContext context) {
  showDialog(
    context: context,
    builder: (BuildContext context) {
      return SimpleDialog(
        title: Text('Choose an Option'),
        children: <Widget>[
          SimpleDialogOption(
            onPressed: () {
              Navigator.pop(context, 'Option 1');
            },
            child: Text('Option 1'),
          ),
          SimpleDialogOption(
            onPressed: () {
              Navigator.pop(context, 'Option 2');
            },
            child: Text('Option 2'),
          ),
          SimpleDialogOption(
            onPressed: () {
              Navigator.pop(context, 'Option 3');
            },
            child: Text('Option 3'),
          ),
        ],
      );
    },
  );
}
```

Key Points

- **Non-Intrusive Overlays:** Simple dialogs appear as compact overlays on top of the current screen, allowing users to interact with them without losing sight of the main app content.
- **Context-Specific Interactions:** Simple dialogs offer relevant choices or input options based on the current screen or user action, providing context-specific interactions.
- **Lightweight and Customizable:** Flutter allows developers to customize the appearance and behaviour of simple dialogs, including colours, fonts, and button styles, to match the app's design.

Benefits of Using Simple Dialogs

- **Enhanced User Interaction:** Simple dialogs provide a seamless way for users to make selections or provide input, improving the overall user experience.
- **Streamlined Navigation:** By presenting context-specific options, simple dialogs help users make decisions without navigating away from their current context.
- **Space-Efficient:** Simple dialogs are compact and space-efficient, making them ideal for presenting a limited set of choices or input fields.

Common Use Cases for Simple Dialogs

- **Confirmation Dialogs:** Simple dialogs can prompt users to confirm or cancel critical actions, such as deleting items or submitting sensitive data.
- **Option Selection:** When users need to make a choice from a list of options, simple dialogs provide a concise and clear way to present those choices.
- **Input Forms:** Simple dialogs are useful for collecting user input, such as entering text, selecting dates, or choosing from a list of predefined values.

Alert Dialogs

Alert dialogs are a crucial component in Flutter that enables developers to present critical information or seek user confirmation through overlay windows. These dialogs are lightweight, non-intrusive, and provide a straightforward way to interact with uscrs without navigating to a new screen. Alert dialogs are commonly used to display important messages, notifications, or to prompt users for confirmation before performing significant actions.

In this section, we will explore the basics of alert dialogs, their benefits, and provide examples of how to create and customize them in Flutter.

Key Points

- **Non-Intrusive Information Display:** Alert dialogs appear as small overlay windows on top of the current screen, ensuring that users can easily read and acknowledge the information without disrupting their workflow.
- **Versatility and Customizability:** Flutter allows developers to customize the content, appearance, and actions of alert dialogs to match the app's design and branding.
- **Multiple Action Buttons:** Alert dialogs can have one or more action buttons, allowing users to confirm or cancel an action with a single tap.
- **User-Friendly Interactions:** Alert dialogs provide a clear and concise way to present critical information or seek user confirmation, leading to a better user experience.

Benefits of Using Alert Dialogs

- **Effective Communication:** Alert dialogs enable developers to communicate important information, such as success messages, errors, or warnings, to users in a visually appealing manner.
- **User Confirmation:** By using alert dialogs for confirmation purposes, users can make informed decisions before proceeding with critical actions, preventing accidental data loss or unintended consequences.
- **Space-Efficient Design:** Alert dialogs are compact and space-efficient, making them suitable for displaying brief messages or simple user interactions.

Common Use Cases for Alert Dialogs

- **Error Alerts:** Alert dialogs can be used to display error messages when unexpected issues occur, helping users understand and rectify the problem.
- **Success Messages:** After completing a task, alert dialogs can show success messages to inform users about successful operations.
- **Confirmation Prompts:** Alert dialogs are commonly used to seek user confirmation before deleting data, submitting a form, or performing any irreversible action.

Example of Creating an Alert Dialog in Flutter:

```
void _showAlertDialog(BuildContext context) {
  showDialog(
    context: context,
    builder: (BuildContext context) {
      return AlertDialog(
        title: Text('Alert Dialog'),
        content: Text('This is an example of an alert dialog.'),
        actions: [
          TextButton(
            onPressed: () {
              Navigator.pop(context); // Close the dialog.
            },
            child: Text('OK'),
          ),
        ],
      );
    },
  );
}
```

CupertinoAlertDialog

CupertinoAlertDialog is a specialized type of alert dialog widget in Flutter that follows the design patterns of Apple's iOS. It provides a native look and feel, making it a great choice for iOS app development. CupertinoAlertDialog is part of the Cupertino widget library, which mimics the visual style of iOS components and offers a seamless experience for iOS users.

In this section, we will explore the basics of CupertinoAlertDialog, its key features, and provide examples to demonstrate its usage in Flutter apps.

Key Features of CupertinoAlertDialog

- **Native iOS Look:** CupertinoAlertDialog follows Apple's Human Interface Guidelines, ensuring that it integrates seamlessly with other iOS components, providing an authentic experience for iOS users.
- **Customizable Actions:** CupertinoAlertDialog allows developers to add custom actions, such as buttons, to prompt user interactions, providing flexibility in capturing user input or obtaining confirmation.

- **Simplified Design:** CupertinoAlertDialog provides a straightforward design with a title, content, and action buttons, making it ideal for displaying information or seeking user input without overwhelming the user.

Benefits of Using CupertinoAlertDialog

- **Consistent iOS Experience:** By utilizing CupertinoAlertDialog, developers can create iOS apps that maintain a consistent look and feel, enhancing the user experience for iOS users.
- **Easy Adoption:** For developers familiar with iOS app development, using CupertinoAlertDialog will feel intuitive, as it closely resembles the native iOS alert dialogs.
- **Seamless Integration:** CupertinoAlertDialog integrates smoothly with other Cupertino widgets, allowing for easy integration within the app's UI.

Example of Creating a CupertinoAlertDialog in Flutter:

```
void _showCupertinoAlertDialog(BuildContext context) {
  showCupertinoDialog(
    context: context,
    builder: (BuildContext context) {
      return CupertinoAlertDialog(
        title: Text('Cupertino Alert Dialog'),
        content: Text('This is an example of a CupertinoAlertDialog.'),
        actions: [
          CupertinoDialogAction(
            onPressed: () {
              Navigator.pop(context); // Close the dialog.
            },
            child: Text('OK'),
          ),
        ],
      );
    },
  );
}
```

BottomSheet

BottomSheet is a fundamental UI element in Flutter that appears as a slide-up panel from the bottom of the screen. It is commonly used to display additional content, settings, or user actions that are contextually relevant to the current screen. BottomSheet provides a non-intrusive and space-efficient way to present information or actions without navigating to a new screen.

In this section, we will explore the basics of BottomSheet, its key features, and provide examples to demonstrate its usage in Flutter apps.

Key Features of BottomSheet

- **Slide-Up Panel:** BottomSheet slides smoothly into view from the bottom of the screen, allowing users to interact with it while still viewing the underlying content.
- **Versatile Design:** Flutter allows developers to customize the appearance and behaviour of BottomSheet to match the app's design and branding.
- **Dismissible:** By default, BottomSheet can be dismissed by swiping it down or tapping outside the panel, making it easy for users to close it.

Benefits of Using BottomSheet

- **Space-Efficient:** BottomSheet's slide-up design ensures that it does not take up valuable screen real estate, making it ideal for displaying additional information without obstructing the user's view.
- **Contextually Relevant:** BottomSheet is perfect for displaying actions or content that are contextually relevant to the current screen, improving the user experience by reducing navigation.
- **Seamless Integration:** BottomSheet integrates smoothly with other Flutter widgets, making it easy to add to your app's UI.

  Example of Using BottomSheet in Flutter:

```
void _showBottomSheet(BuildContext context) {
  showModalBottomSheet(
    context: context,
    builder: (BuildContext context) {
      return Container(
        height: 200,
        child: Column(
          children: [
```

```
                ListTile(
                  leading: Icon(Icons.share),
                  title: Text('Share'),
                  onTap: () {
                    // Perform share action.
                    Navigator.pop(context); // Close the bottom sheet.
                  },
                ),
                ListTile(
                  leading: Icon(Icons.delete),
                  title: Text('Delete'),
                  onTap: () {
                    // Perform delete action.
                    Navigator.pop(context); // Close the bottom sheet.
                  },
                ),
              ],
            ),
          );
        },
      );
    }
```

Conclusion

Navigation and routing are important aspects of building any mobile application. Flutter provides us with powerful navigation tools like Navigator, named routes, and model dialogs that make the development process a lot easier. With named routes, we can easily navigate between different screens without worrying about the implementation details. Additionally, using model dialogs, we can prompt users with alerts and gather necessary information from them. These tools are a great way to create a user-friendly application that provides a seamless experience to the users. By mastering these concepts, we can create professional-looking applications with ease.

In the next chapter, we will dive into Firebase Firestore, a real-time NoSQL cloud-based database service provided by Google. We will discuss how to create a Firebase project, add the Firebase plugin to your Flutter project, and implement CRUD (Create, Read, Update, Delete) functions in your app. Additionally, we will explore how to use listeners to keep your app data up-to-date in real-time with Firestore.

Task

Continuing from the previous task, complete the following. In case you could not get through we you can access our GitHub repository (**https://github.com/lahirunc/task_tracker**) and get the solution.

1. Inside the FloatingActionButton onPressed() function, write the code to navigate to CreateTaskScreen.
2. Inside CreateTaskScreen, return a Scaffold and move Center widget inside its body. Content in the Text widget inside the Center should be changed to “Create Task Body” .
3. Add an AppBar widget to the Scaffold inside the CreateTaskScreen and title as “Create Task”.

Questions

1. **What is the purpose of the Flutter Navigator?**
    a. To manage screen navigation in a Flutter application
    b. To manage widget layouts in a Flutter application
    c. To manage data storage in a Flutter application
    d. To manage user authentication in a Flutter application
2. **What is a named route in Flutter?**
    a. A route with a specific name assigned to it
    b. A route that can only be accessed by a specific user
    c. A route that requires authentication to access
    d. A route that contains specific data for the user
3. **How do you navigate to a named route in Flutter?**
    a. Using the `Navigator.push()` method
    b. Using the `Navigator.pushReplacement()` method
    c. Using the `Navigator.pushNamed()` method
    d. Using the `Navigator.pop()` method

4. **How do you navigate back to the previous screen using the Navigator in Flutter?**
    a. Using the **`Navigator.push()`** method
    b. Using the **`Navigator.pushReplacement()`** method
    c. Using the **`Navigator.pushNamed()`** method
    d. Using the **`Navigator.pop()`** method

5. **Can you pass data back to the previous screen using the Navigator in Flutter?**
    a. Yes, by using the **`Navigator.push()`** method
    b. Yes, by using the **`Navigator.pushNamed()`** method
    c. Yes, by using the **`Navigator.pop()`** method with a result parameter
    d. No, it is not possible to pass data back using the Navigator

6. **What is a model dialog in Flutter**
    a. A widget that is always open
    b. A dialog that takes up the entire screen and blocks all other input
    c. A dialog that can be dismissed without user interaction
    d. A widget that is only open when called by another widget

7. **Which of the following is not a type of dialog in Flutter?**
    a. AlertDialog
    b. CupertinoDialog
    c. SimpleDialog
    d. NotificationDialog

8. **How do you show a SimpleDialog in Flutter?**
    a. Using the **`showDialog()`** function
    b. Using the **`showSimpleDialog()`** function
    c. Using the **`showModalDialog()`** function
    d. SimpleDialog cannot be shown in Flutter

9. **How do you dismiss a dialog in Flutter**
    a. By calling the **`Navigator.pop()`** function
    b. By calling the **`showDialog()`** function
    c. By calling the **`setState()`** function
    d. By calling the **`dismiss()`** function

Answers

1. **a**
2. **a**
3. **c**
4. **d**
5. **c**
6. **b**
7. **d**
8. **a**
9. **a**

Reference

- **https://docs.flutter.dev/development/ui/navigation**

CHAPTER 6
Firebase Firestore with Flutter

Introduction

In this chapter, we will discuss the basics of Firebase Firestore and how to use it in a Flutter app. We will learn how to create a Firebase project, add the Firebase Firestore plugin to our Flutter project, and perform basic CRUD (Create, Read, Update, Delete) operations with Firestore. Additionally, we will explore the use of Firestore listeners to update our UI in real-time as data changes in the database.

By the end of this chapter, you will have a solid understanding of how to use Firebase Firestore in your Flutter apps to manage and synchronize data, and how to integrate it with other Firebase services to build powerful and feature-rich applications.

Structure

In this chapter, we will cover the following topics:

- Introduction to Firebase Firestore
- Creating your Firebase project
- Adding Firebase to Flutter
- CRUD functions
- Listeners

Introduction to Firebase Firestore

Firebase Firestore is a cloud-based NoSQL document database provided by Google as part of the Firebase platform. It allows developers to store, sync, and query data for their applications. Firestore offers real-time data synchronization, which means that any changes made to the data are automatically propagated to all connected clients in real-time.

Firestore organizes data into collections and documents. A collection is a group of related documents, while each document contains a set of key-value pairs called fields. Documents are uniquely identified within a collection and can be accessed using their document ID.

Firestore provides a powerful querying mechanism that allows developers to retrieve data based on various criteria. Queries can filter, sort, and paginate data, enabling efficient data retrieval and manipulation. Firestore also supports composite indexes to optimize query performance.

One of the key features of Firestore is its real-time data synchronization. Any changes made to the database, either from the client-side or server-side, are instantly reflected in all connected clients. This enables real-time collaboration, live updates, and interactive features in applications.

Firestore integrates seamlessly with other Firebase services, such as Firebase Authentication for user authentication and Firebase Cloud Functions for serverless backend logic. It also provides SDKs for various platforms, including Flutter, making it easy to integrate Firestore into your Flutter applications.

In Flutter, you can use the cloud_firestore package to interact with Firestore. This package provides classes and methods to perform CRUD operations, listen for real-time updates, and manage data using Firestore's powerful query capabilities.

Overall, Firebase Firestore simplifies the process of storing and synchronizing data in the cloud for your Flutter applications. It offers scalability, real-time synchronization, and a flexible querying system, making it a popular choice for building data-driven and collaborative applications.

Creating your Firebase project

Creating a Firebase project is a crucial step in building any app that requires cloud-based services. Firebase is a powerful platform that provides numerous tools and services to make your app development process easier and faster. Firebase Firestore is a NoSQL document-based database that is used to store and manage data in real-time.

To get started with Firebase Firestore, you first need to create a Firebase project. Follow these simple steps to create your Firebase project:

1. Go to the Firebase Console. Visit the Firebase Console by typing **https://console.firebase.google.com/** in your browser (*Figure* 6.1).

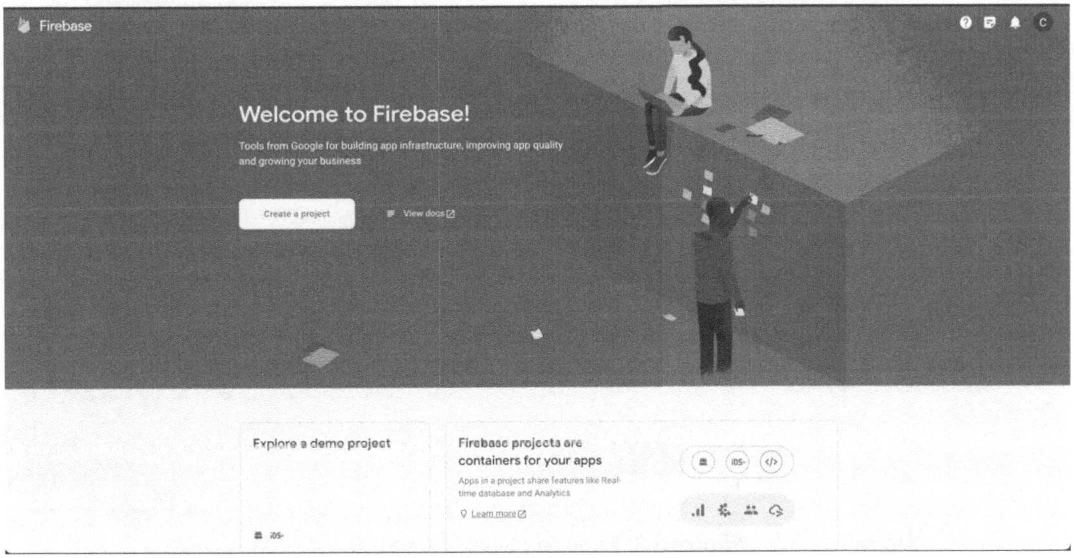

Figure 6.1: *Firebase Firestore Home Page* **(https://console.firebase.google.com)**

2. Click on the `Create Project` button to create a new Firebase project (*Figure* 6.1). You will be asked to provide a project name (*Figure* 6.2).

Figure 6.2: *Creating a project*

You can also choose to enable Google Analytics (*Figure* 6.3 and *Figure* 6.4) for your project.

Figure 6.3 shows the enabling Google Analytics.

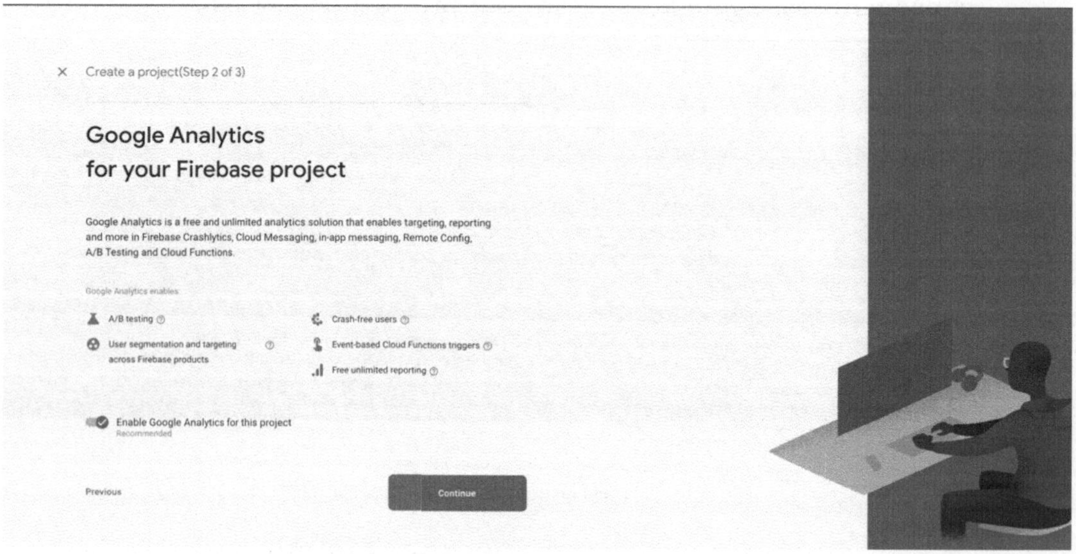

Figure 6.3: *Enabling Google Analytics*

Figure 6.4 shows and configuring of Google Analytics:

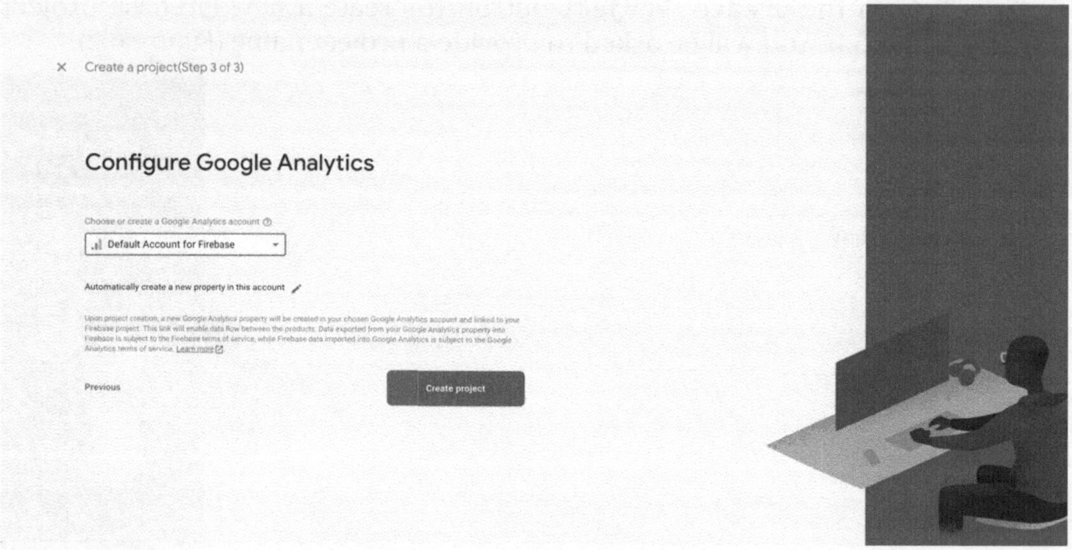

Figure 6.4: *Configuring Google Analytics*

1. Once you've created your project, you need to enable Firestore. To do this, go to the `Firestore` tab in the Firebase console and click on the `Create Database` button (*Figure 6.5*).

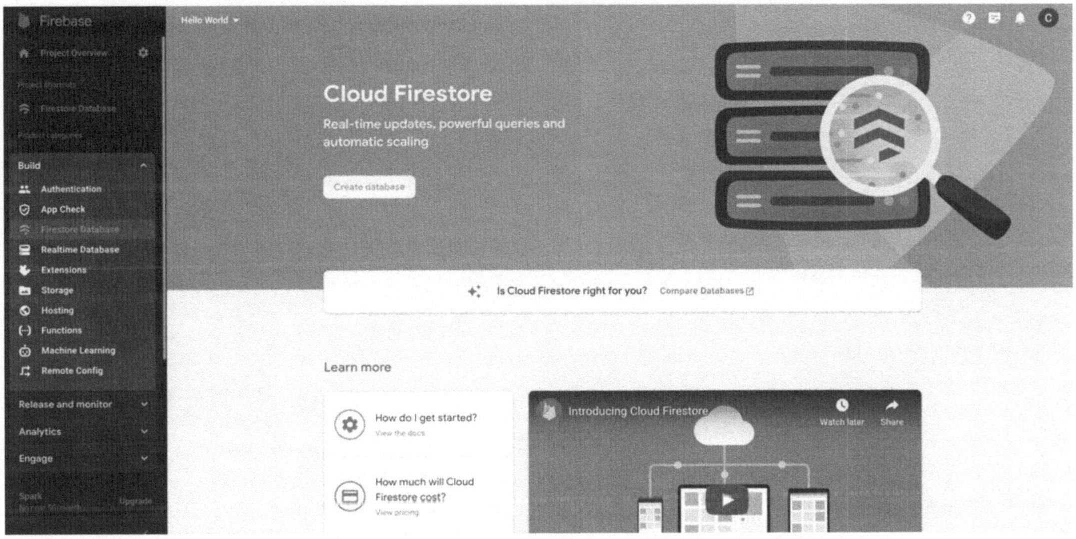

Figure 6.5: *Firebase Firestore Enabling*

2. Configure your Firestore Security Rules to ensure that only authorized users can access your data. You can choose to start with test rules and refine them later (*Figure 6.6*).

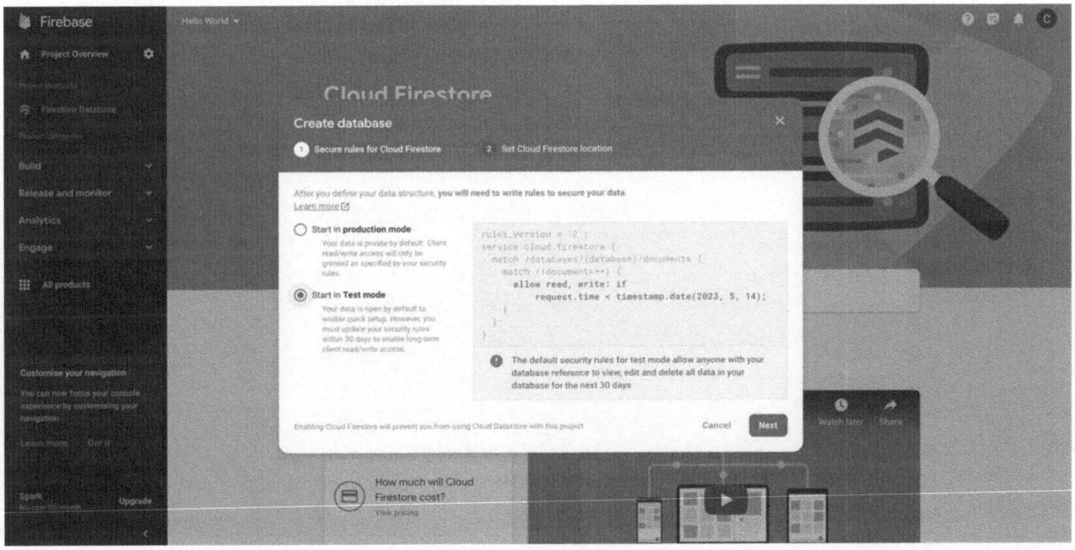

Figure 6.6: *Firebase Firestore Rules*

3. You can choose the location of your Cloud Firestore data that will be stored. Click on the "Dropdown" and select the location you desire. Then click "Enable" (*Figure 6.7*).

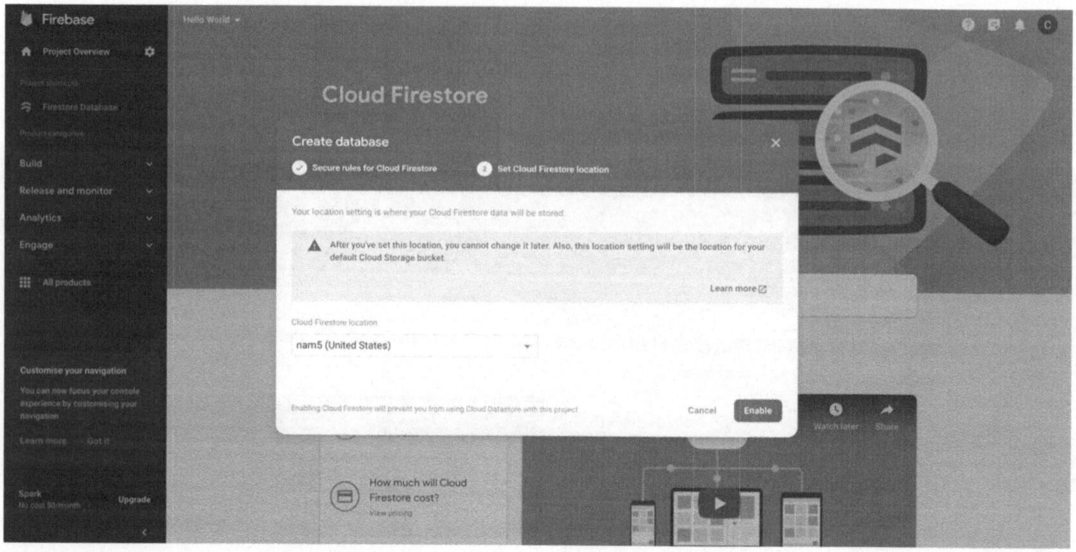

Figure 6.7: *Set Cloud Firestore location*

Once you've completed these steps, you will have successfully created your Firebase project and enabled Firestore. You're now ready to start building your app and using Firestore to store and manage your data.

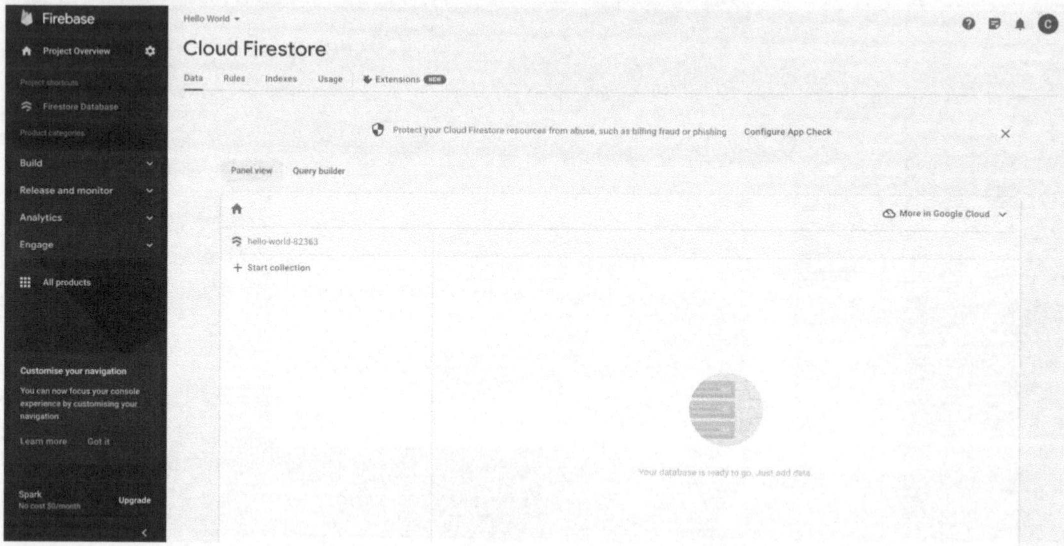

Figure 6.8: *Firebase Firestore Database*

Adding Firebase to Flutter

Before starting, you need to have a Firebase project with Firestore enabled, and a Flutter project. If you don't have them, you can create them by following the instructions in the previous chapters. You can get it done by following these steps:

1. To use Firebase Firestore in your Flutter project, you need to add "firebase_core" (*Figure* 6.9) and "cloud_firestore" dependencies to your pubspec.yaml file.

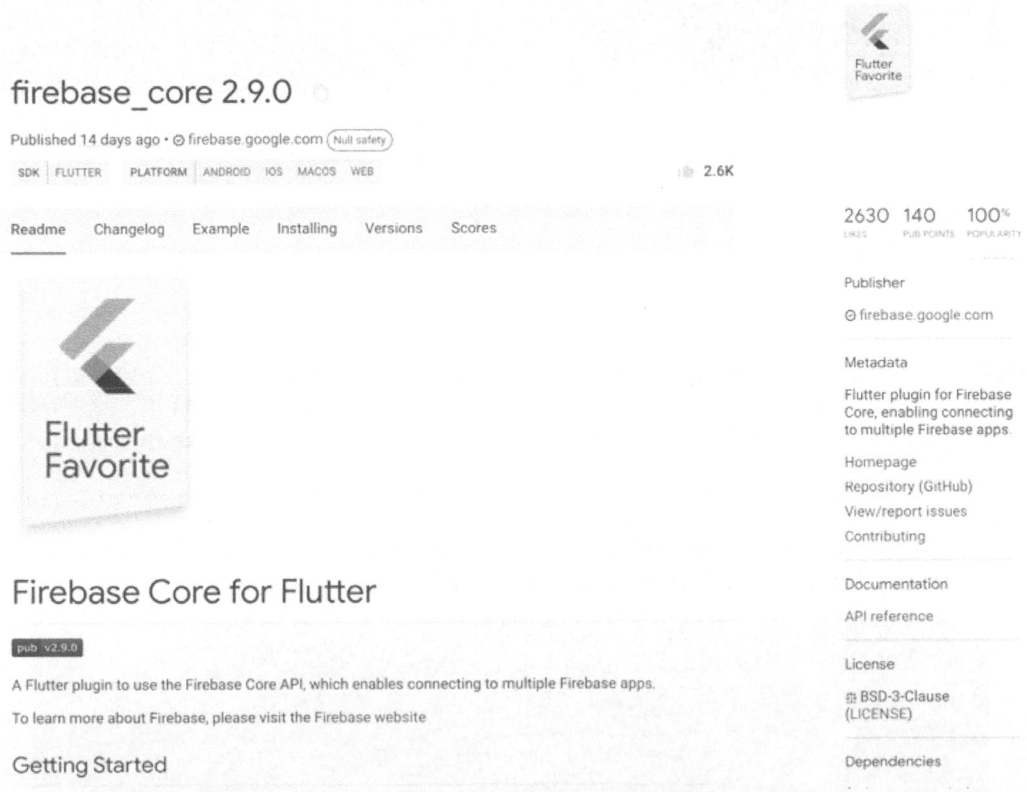

Figure 6.9: *firebase_core package*

You can find Flutter dependencies from pub.dev (https://pub.dev) (*Figure 6.10*).

Figure 6.10: *pub.dev home page*

Tip: You can use **Pubspec Assist by Jeroen Meijer** (*https://marketplace.visualstudio.com/items?itemName=jeroen-meijer.pubspec-assist*) extension *which can be installed in VS Code to install packages easily just by typing the name.*

2. Next, create a Flutter app inside the Firebase by clicking **`Project Overview`** and clicking on Flutter Icon (*Figure 6.11*).

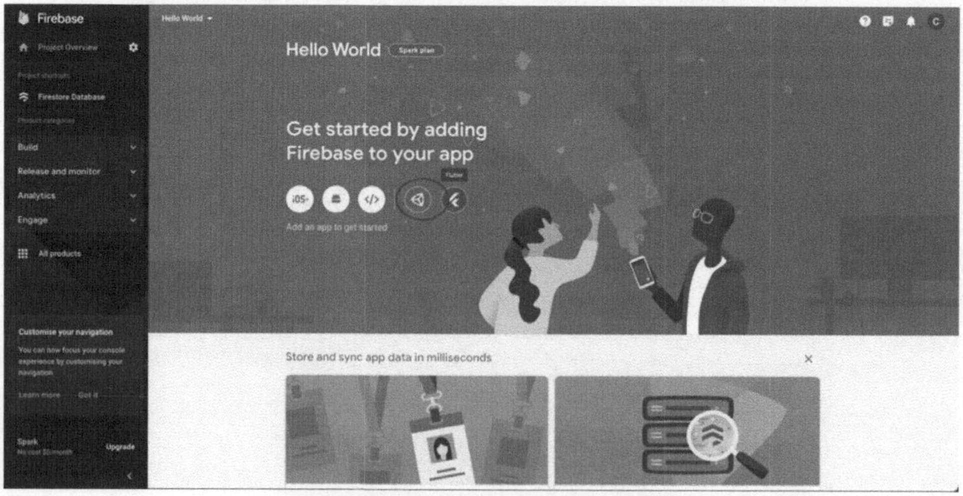

Figure 6.11: *Firebase Project Overview*

3. Follow the instructions on the “**`Add Firebase to your Flutter app`**" page. This includes installing FlutterFire CLI (***https://firebase.google.com/docs/cli***), and activating FlutterFire CLI using the following command in the terminal:

   ```
   dart pub global activate flutterfire_cli
   ```

4. Run the following command in your Flutter project root

   ```
   flutterfire configure --project=<PROJECT_NAME>
   ```

5. Finally, update the main.dart file

   ```
   Future<void> main() async {
     WidgetsFlutterBinding.ensureInitialized();
     await Firebase.initializeApp(
       options: DefaultFirebaseOptions.currentPlatform,
     );
     runApp(const MyApp());
   }
   ```

We have learned how to add Firebase to a Flutter project and specifically how to integrate Firebase Firestore. By following the steps outlined, we have successfully created a Firebase project and added it to our Flutter app.

CRUD Functions

Understanding the Firebase Firestore Structure

In Firestore, data is organized into collections and documents. Collections can contain multiple documents, and each document contains a set of key-value pairs. In this blog post, we'll dive deeper into collections and documents in Firebase Firestore.

- **Collections**

  A collection is a container for a group of documents. It is similar to a table in a traditional SQL database. Each collection can have multiple documents, and each document can have different fields and values. Collections can be nested, meaning a collection can be a sub-collection of another collection.

- **Documents**

  A document is a set of key-value pairs stored in a collection. It is similar to a row in a traditional SQL database. Each document has a unique identifier, which is automatically generated by Firebase Firestore. Documents can be organized into collections based on their type or purpose.

Firestore supports various field types, allowing you to store different kinds of data. Some common field types include:

- **Strings:** Storing text or character data.
- **Numbers:** Storing numeric values such as integers or decimals.
- **Booleans:** Storing true or false values.
- **Dates and Timestamps:** Storing date and time information.
- **Arrays:** Storing ordered lists of values.
- **Maps:** Storing nested data structures.
- **References:** Storing references to other documents within Firestore.

You can create new documents in Firestore by specifying a unique document identifier within a collection. Each document can have multiple fields, and you can update or modify these fields as needed. Firestore provides flexible APIs and SDKs to interact with documents programmatically.

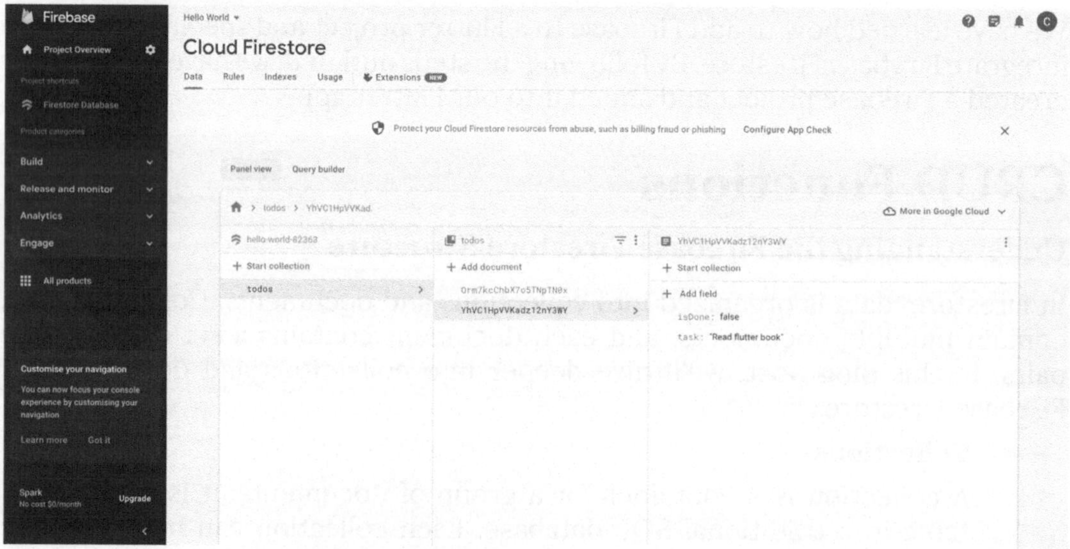

Figure 6.12: Firebase Firestore Collections and Documents

Using Firebase Firestore

To use the Firestore database, we need to create an instance of it. We can do this by adding the following line of code:

```
final FirebaseFirestore firestore = FirebaseFirestore.instance;
```

Now that we have set up Firebase Firestore in our Flutter application, we can start performing CRUD operations. Let's discuss each of these operations one by one.

Create

To create a new document in Firebase Firestore, we can use the following code:

```
firestore.collection("collection_name").doc().set({
  "field_name": "field_value",
});
```

Read

Get all documents

To retrieve all documents in a collection, you can use the get() method on the collection reference. This returns a QuerySnapshot containing all the documents.

```
firestore.collection("todos").get().then((QuerySnapshot snapshot) {
  snapshot.docs.forEach((DocumentSnapshot doc) {
    print(doc);
  });
});
```

Filtering documents

You can filter documents based on specific criteria using the where() method. For example (refer to *Figure* 6.12), to retrieve only completed todos, you can use the following query.

```
firestore.collection("todos").where('isDone',isEqualTo: true).get().
then((QuerySnapshot snapshot) {
  snapshot.docs.forEach((DocumentSnapshot doc) {
    print(doc);
  });
});
```

Ordering documents

You can also order the retrieved documents based on a specific field using the orderBy() method. For example (*Figure* 6.12), to retrieve todos ordered by the task description, you can use the following query:

```
firestore.collection("todos").orderBy('task').get().then((QuerySnapshot
snapshot) {
  snapshot.docs.forEach((DocumentSnapshot doc) {
    print(doc);
  });
});
```

Limiting the number of documents

If you only need a limited number of documents, you can use the **limit()** method. For example (*Figure* 6.12), to retrieve the first 5 todos, you can use the following query:

```
firestore.collection("todos").limit(5).get().then((QuerySnapshot
snapshot) {
  snapshot.docs.forEach((DocumentSnapshot doc) {
    print(doc);
  });
});
```

Update

Updating single document

To update a single document, you need to obtain a reference to that document using its unique key. For example (*Figure* 6.12), if you have a document with the key **YhVC1HpVVKadz12nY3WY** inside the "todos" collection, you can update it as follows:

```
firestore.collection("todos").doc("YhVC1HpVVKadz12nY3WY").update({
  'task': 'Updated task',
  'isDone': true,
}).then((_) {
  print('Document updated successfully!');
}).catchError((error) {
  print('Error updating document: $error');
});
```

Updating multiple documents

To update multiple documents that match a specific condition, you can use the **where()** method to filter documents based on specific criteria. For example (*Figure* 6.12), let's update all documents where the 'isDone' field is false:

```
firestore.collection("todos").where('isDone',isEqualTo: false).get().
then((QuerySnapshot snapshot) {
  snapshot.docs.forEach((DocumentSnapshot doc) {
    DocumentReference docRef = firestore.collection("todos").doc(doc.id);

    docRef.update({
      'isDone': true,
    }).then((_) {
      print('Document updated successfully!');
    }).catchError((error) {
      print('Error updating document: $error');
    });
  });
});
```

In this case, we use the where() method to filter documents where the 'isDone' field is false, and then update the 'isDone' field to true for each matching document.

Delete

Delete a single document

To delete a single document, you need to obtain a reference to that document using its unique key. For example (*Figure* 6.12), if you have a document with the key " YhVC1HpVVKadz12nY3WY " inside the "todos" collection, you can delete it as follows:

```
firestore.collection("todos").doc("YhVC1HpVVKadz12nY3WY").delete().
then((_) {
  print('Document deleted successfully!');
}).catchError((error) {
  print('Error deleting document: $error');
});
```

Delete multiple documents

To delete a single document, you need to obtain a reference to that document using its unique key. For example (*Figure 6.12*), if you have a document with the key **`YhVC1HpVVKadz12nY3WY`** inside the "todos" collection, you can delete it as follows:

```
firestore.collection("todos").where('isDone',isEqualTo: true).get().
then((QuerySnapshot snapshot) {
  snapshot.docs.forEach((DocumentSnapshot doc) {
    DocumentReference docRef = firestore.collection("todos").doc(doc.id);

    docRef.delete().then((_) {
      print('Document deleted successfully!');
    }).catchError((error) {
      print('Error deleting document: $error');
    });
  });
});
```

In this case, we use the **`where()`** method to filter documents where the 'isDone' field is true, and then delete each matching document.

By utilizing the **`delete()`** method along with the **`where()`** method, you can perform delete queries in Firebase Firestore with Flutter. Remember to handle any potential errors that may occur during the deletion process.

Listeners

Firebase Firestore listeners are a powerful tool that allows you to receive real-time updates whenever there is a change in the database. With listeners, you can build reactive and dynamic apps that respond to changes in data in real-time.

Listening to the entire collection

To listen to the entire collection in Firebase Firestore, you can use the snapshots() method on a collection reference. This allows you to receive real-time updates whenever there are changes to any document within the collection. Let's explore how to listen to the entire collection with additional filtering and limiting options:

Listening to the entire collection

To listen to the entire collection, you can use the snapshots() method on a collection reference. This returns a Stream<**QuerySnapshot**> that emits a stream of snapshots containing the current state of the documents in the collection. For example (*Figure* 6.12):

```
StreamSubscription<QuerySnapshot> subscription= firestore.
collection("todos").snapshots().listen((QuerySnapshot snapshot) {
  snapshot.docs.forEach((DocumentSnapshot doc) {
    // Access the document data
    Map<String, dynamic> data = doc.data();
    // Process the data as needed
    print(data);
  });
});

// Don't forget to cancel the subscription when no longer needed
subscription.cancel();
```

Adding filters and limiting results

You can also apply filters and limits to the collection query to retrieve only specific documents. For example (*Figure* 6.12), let's listen to only those documents where the 'isDone' field is true and limit the results to 5:

```
StreamSubscription<QuerySnapshot> subscription= firestore.
collection("todos").where('isDone', isEqualTo: true)
    .limit(5)
    .snapshots()
    .listen((QuerySnapshot snapshot) {
  snapshot.docs.forEach((DocumentSnapshot doc) {
    // Access the filtered document data
    Map<String, dynamic> data = doc.data();
    // Process the data as needed
    print(data);
  });
});
```

```
// Don't forget to cancel the subscription when no longer needed
subscription.cancel();
```

In this case, we apply the **`where()`** method to filter documents where the 'isDone' field is true and use the limit() method to restrict the results to 5 documents.

By utilizing the **`snapshots()`** method along with the **`where()`**, **`limit()`**, and other query methods, you can listen to the entire collection with additional filtering and limiting options in Firebase Firestore with Flutter. Remember to handle any potential errors and cancel the subscription when no longer needed to prevent unnecessary data listening.

Listening to the selected document

To listen to a selected collection in Firebase Firestore, you can use the snapshots() method on a query reference with specified filters and limits. This allows you to receive real-time updates for the selected documents that match your criteria. Let's explore how to listen to a selected collection with additional filtering and limiting options:

Listening to a selected collection

To listen to a selected collection, you need to create a query reference using the where() method on a collection reference. This allows you to specify the criteria for selecting the documents. For example (*Figure* 6.12):

```
StreamSubscription<QuerySnapshot> subscription = firestore.
collection("todos")
    .where('isDone', isEqualTo: true)
    .snapshots()
    .listen((QuerySnapshot snapshot) {
  snapshot.docs.forEach((DocumentSnapshot doc) {
    // Access the selected document data
    Map<String, dynamic> data = doc.data();
    // Process the data as needed
    print(data);
  });
});


// Don't forget to cancel the subscription when no longer needed
subscription.cancel();
```

In this example, we listen to changes in the "todos" collection and retrieve only those documents where the 'isDone' field is true.

Adding filters and limiting results

You can further refine the selection by applying additional filters and limits to the query. For example (*Figure* 6.12), let's listen to the selected documents where 'isDone' is true, 'priority' is greater than or equal to 2, and limit the results to 5:

```
StreamSubscription<QuerySnapshot> subscription = firestore.
collection("todos").where('isDone', isEqualTo: true)
    .where('priority', isGreaterThanOrEqualTo: 2)
    .limit(5)
    .snapshots()
    .listen((QuerySnapshot snapshot) {
  snapshot.docs.forEach((DocumentSnapshot doc) {
    // Access the filtered document data
    Map<String, dynamic> data = doc.data();
    // Process the data as needed
    print(data);
  });
});

// Don't forget to cancel the subscription when no longer needed
subscription.cancel();
```

In this case, we apply the where() method multiple times to add filters based on the 'isDone' and 'priority' fields, and use the limit() method to restrict the results to 5 documents.

By utilizing the snapshots() method along with the where(), limit(), and other query methods, you can listen to a selected collection with specified filters and limits in Firebase Firestore with Flutter. Remember to handle any potential errors and cancel the subscription when no longer needed to prevent unnecessary data listening.

Conclusion

Firebase Firestore is a powerful database solution that integrates well with Flutter applications. In this chapter, we learned about creating a Firebase project, adding Firebase Firestore to our Flutter project, and using CRUD operations to manipulate data. We also explored the concept of collections and documents and how to work with them in Firestore.

In the next chapter, we will dive deeper into asynchronous programming in Flutter and explore Futures, awaits, and async functions, which are essential for working with Firebase Firestore listeners and other asynchronous operations in Flutter.

Task

Continuing from the previous task, complete the following. In case you cannot get through you can access our GitHub repository (**https://github.com/lahirunc/task_tracker**) and get the solution. Each task has its specific branch.

Moving forward, the instructions may seem complicated. Therefore, the book will be providing you with the entire code snippets, but we encourage you to figure out and use snippets and repositories as the last resort. Try to do some trial and error. If an error is found, try doing a Google search. You'll find many just like you and me having asked for help from others in the community.

1. Get your Flutter app connected to Firebase Firestore.
2. Let's create our first form. Inside the "CreateTaskScreen", Replace Center and Text widget with a Form widget.
3. Add a Column as a child inside the Form widget and wrap it around a Padding widget.

```
Form(
        child: Padding(
          padding: const EdgeInsets.all(8.0),
          child: Column(
          children: [],
    ),
        ),
      ),
```

Note: In Flutter, the Padding widget is used to add padding (empty space) around its child widget. Padding can be added to any side of the child widget or all sides. The Padding widget is useful for adding space between widgets, providing visual breathing room and improving readability of the UI. It can also be used to align child widgets within a parent widget.

4. Next, to validate the Form, create a GlobalKey<FormState> named formKey before the build(BuildContext context) function.

```
final GlobalKey<FormState> formKey = GlobalKey<FormState>();
```

5. Add the following as we will be using our first **TextFormField** before the **build(BuildContext context)** function. **TextEditingController** is used to listen to value inside the **TextFormField**.

```
final TextEditingController textEditingController =
TextEditingController();
```

6. Then add formKey inside the Form.

```
 Form(
    key: formKey
          child: Padding(
          padding: const EdgeInsets.all(8.0),
          child: Column(
          children: [],
   ),
        ),
      ),
```

7. Inside the Column, add two widgets TextFormField and ElevatedButton named Create. Also, add MainAxisAlignment.center inside the Column.

```
Form(
        // add the formKey here
        key: formKey,
        child: Padding(
          padding: const EdgeInsets.all(8.0),
          child: Column(
            mainAxisAlignment: MainAxisAlignment.center,
            children: [
              TextFormField(),
              ElevatedButton(
                child: const Text('Create'),
                onPressed: () {},
              ),
            ],
```

```
          ),
        ),
      ),
```

8. Add **textEditingController** to **TextFormField** and we will also add validation to check if the TextFormField is empty.

```
TextFormField(
                // add text textEditingController here.
                controller: textEditingController,
                // validator is used to validate the data.
                validator: (String? value) {
                  // here you can check if the value is empty and
                  // show a message to stop the user from
creating
                  // empty or null records .
                  if (value == null || value.isEmpty) {
                    return 'Cannot be empty!';
                  }
                  return null;
                },
              ),
```

9. Next, we'll validate the form and if the TextFormField is not empty save the value in the TextFormField with a key named as task along with another key status with a value false to the Firebase Firestore.

```
ElevatedButton(
                child: const Text('Create'),
                onPressed: () {
                  // if the form is valid then it will return true,
                  // else false.
                  if (formKey.currentState!.validate()) {
                    // create query for the task
                    FirebaseFirestore.instance.
                          collection('tasks').doc().set({
                      'task': textEditingController.text,
                      'status': false,
```

```
                    });
                  }
                },
              ),
```

The final result (*Figure* 6.13) of the task can be via this link **https://github.com/lahirunc/task_tracker/blob/Task-3/lib/screens/create_task_screen.dart**

Figure 6.13: *Final look of the CreateTaskScreen*

10. Let's create a listener to read all tasks. Convert the HomeScreen into StatefulWidget.

Tip: You can use Code Actions in VS Code to convert it easily. Move your cursor to the line "class HomeScreen extends StatelessWidget" line. Then click on the bulb icon and select* `Convert to StatefulWidget` *(Figure 6.14):

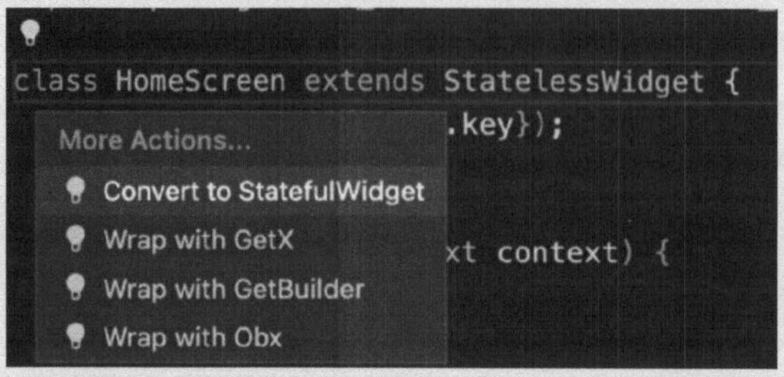

Figure 6.14: *Code Actions*

11. Add **`initState()`** listener between _HomeScreenState and build() function. Inside the initState() function add Firebase Firestore listener.

```
final FirebaseFirestore firestore = FirebaseFirestore.instance;


  @override
  void initState() {
    firestore.collection("tasks").snapshots().
listen((QuerySnapshot event) {
      for (var task in event.docs) {
        print(task.data());
      }
    });


    super.initState();
  }
```

Note: `initState()` is a method in the stateful widget in Flutter that is called once when the widget is inserted into the widget tree. It is typically used to initialize the state of the widget. This method is called only once during the lifecycle of the widget and is used to set up the widget's initial state. It is often used to perform any one-time initialization tasks, such as initializing variables or setting up listeners, that are required for the widget to function correctly.

12. Finally, create the following UI shown in Figure 6.15 inside the HomeScreen Scaffold body.

Tip: *Have a look into Card, ListTile, and Checkbox*

Figure 6.15: *Home Screen Task Widget*

13. If you're adventurous, we like you to populate the task you have added to the screen. You can use the StreamBuilder and ListView.builder.

Multiple Choice Questions

1. **What is Firebase Firestore?**
    a. A real-time database
    b. A NoSQL document-based database
    c. A SQL database
    d. A relational database

2. **What is the difference between a collection and a document in Firebase Firestore?**
    a. Collection is a group of documents and documents are individual records.
    b. Document is a group of collections and collections are individual records.
    c. Collection and document are the same thing.
    d. None of the above

3. **What is the primary benefit of using Firebase Firestore in a Flutter app?**
    a. It provides a built-in user authentication system.
    b. It allows you to easily store and retrieve data from a cloud-based database.
    c. It offers pre-built UI widgets for common app features.
    d. It simplifies the process of deploying your app to the app store.

4. **In Firebase Firestore, a collection is:**
    a. A single document within a database.
    b. A group of documents with similar data.
    c. A set of fields within a document.
    d. A unique identifier for a document.

5. **What is the purpose of listeners in Firebase Firestore?**
    a. To display data in real-time as it is updated in the database
    b. To perform complex queries on the data
    c. To secure the data from unauthorized access
    d. To create backup copies of the data.

Answers

1. b
2. a
3. b
4. b
5. a

References

- **https://firebase.google.com/docs/cli**
- **https://docs.flutter.dev/development/packages-and-plugins/using-packages**
- **https://docs.flutter.dev/cookbook/forms/validation**

CHAPTER 7
Futures, Awaits, and Async

Introduction

Welcome to the chapter on Futures, Awaits, and Asyncs in Flutter. In any programming language, there are times when the execution of a piece of code can take a long time to complete, and during that time, the application may not be responsive to user interactions. This can lead to a poor user experience and can be frustrating for users.

To solve this problem, Flutter provides Futures, Awaits, and Asyncs. These are powerful tools that allow you to execute long-running operations in the background without blocking the main UI thread. This means that the user interface remains responsive while the operation is executing, and the user can continue to interact with the app.

In this chapter, we will explore how to use Futures, Awaits, and Asyncs in Flutter. We will cover the basics of how they work, and then dive into some practical examples of how they can be used in real-world applications. We will also cover some best practices for using these tools effectively, as well as some common pitfalls to avoid.

By the end of this chapter, you will have a solid understanding of how to use Futures, Awaits, and Asyncs in your Flutter applications, and you will be able to write code that is both responsive and efficient. So, let's get started!

Structure

In this chapter, we will cover the following topics:

- Understanding Asynchronous Programming
- Futures
- Await
- Async

Understanding Asynchronous Programming

Asynchronous programming is a fundamental concept in Flutter development that allows applications to perform time-consuming tasks without blocking the user interface. By leveraging asynchronous programming, developers can ensure that their apps remain responsive and provide a smooth user experience, even when executing operations that may take some time to complete.

In traditional synchronous programming, each line of code is executed one after the other, and the program waits for each operation to finish before moving on to the next. However, in mobile app development, tasks like making network requests, accessing databases, or performing complex computations can introduce significant delays, potentially causing the app to become unresponsive or freeze.

To overcome this limitation, Flutter utilizes asynchronous programming techniques, which enable multiple operations to run concurrently. This means that the app can continue executing other tasks while waiting for time-consuming operations to complete. Asynchronous programming allows developers to offload resource-intensive tasks to separate threads or processes, ensuring that the user interface remains responsive and interactive.

Flutter provides a powerful set of tools and language features to support asynchronous programming. One of the key concepts is the use of Futures. A Future is a placeholder object that represents a value that may not be available yet. It allows developers to initiate a task and receive the result later. By using Futures, developers can initiate asynchronous operations and handle the results or errors once they become available.

To work with Futures, Flutter introduces the await and async keywords. The await keyword allows developers to pause the execution of a function until a Future completes, while the async keyword indicates that a function can use the await keyword internally. These keywords make it easier to write asynchronous code that resembles synchronous code in terms of readability and structure.

Asynchronous programming in Flutter offers several benefits. It enhances the user experience by ensuring that the app remains responsive, even when performing complex operations. It allows for efficient resource utilization by running tasks concurrently. Additionally, it enables developers to write more maintainable and readable code by handling asynchronous operations in a structured and intuitive manner.

The need for asynchronous operations in mobile applications

Mobile applications often require performing tasks that take time to complete, such as making network requests, accessing databases, or processing large amounts of data. These operations can be time-consuming and may cause the application to become unresponsive if executed synchronously. To address this challenge, asynchronous operations are necessary in mobile applications to ensure a smooth user experience and maintain app responsiveness.

One of the primary reasons for using asynchronous operations is to avoid blocking the user interface. In synchronous programming, each operation is executed one after the other, causing the application to wait for each task to finish before proceeding to the next. This approach can lead to frozen or unresponsive interfaces, frustrating users and potentially causing them to abandon the app.

By employing asynchronous operations, mobile applications can continue executing tasks in the background while the user interface remains responsive. For example, when a network request is made asynchronously, the app can display a loading spinner or continue accepting user input without being blocked by the request. This ensures that the user can continue interacting with the app while waiting for the operation to complete.

Asynchronous operations are also crucial for handling time-consuming tasks efficiently. Mobile devices have limited resources, including processing power and network bandwidth. Synchronous execution of resource-intensive tasks can consume significant system resources, slowing down the app and potentially draining the device's battery quickly. By performing such tasks asynchronously, the application can utilize resources more efficiently and provide a better user experience.

Furthermore, asynchronous operations enable parallel execution, allowing multiple tasks to run concurrently. This concurrency can be especially beneficial when dealing with independent operations, such as fetching data from multiple sources or performing calculations on different sets of data. By executing these tasks concurrently, the overall execution time can be significantly reduced, leading to improved app performance and responsiveness.

In conclusion, asynchronous operations are essential in mobile applications to ensure a smooth user experience, prevent the UI from becoming unresponsive, and optimize resource utilization. By leveraging asynchronous programming techniques, developers can handle time-consuming tasks effectively, maintain app responsiveness, and provide an overall better user experience. In the following sections, we will explore the specific tools and techniques available in Flutter for implementing asynchronous operations and harnessing their benefits in mobile app development.

Benefits and challenges of asynchronous programming

Asynchronous programming brings several benefits to the table, but it also comes with its own set of challenges. Let's explore both the benefits and challenges of asynchronous programming in Flutter.

Benefits of Asynchronous Programming

- **Improved App Responsiveness**: By executing time-consuming tasks asynchronously, the application can remain responsive and continue to handle user interactions while waiting for the tasks to complete. This ensures a smooth and uninterrupted user experience.
- **Enhanced Performance**: Asynchronous programming allows for parallel execution of tasks, which can lead to improved performance. By leveraging the power of concurrency, multiple independent operations can run simultaneously, reducing overall execution time and enhancing app performance.
- **Efficient Resource Utilization**: Asynchronous operations enable the efficient utilization of system resources. By performing tasks in the background, the application can optimize the use of processing power, network bandwidth, and other resources, resulting in better resource management and reduced battery consumption.
- **Non-Blocking, I/O**: Asynchronous programming is particularly useful when dealing with I/O operations, such as network requests or database queries. By executing these operations asynchronously, the application can initiate the request and continue executing other tasks without waiting for the I/O operation to complete.

Challenges of Asynchronous Programming

- **Complex Control Flow**: Asynchronous programming introduces a more complex control flow compared to synchronous programming. Managing callbacks, promises, or futures requires careful handling to ensure that tasks are executed in the correct sequence and error handling is properly implemented.
- **Callback Hell and Nested Code**: Asynchronous programming can sometimes lead to nested and hard-to-read code structures, commonly referred to as **callback hell**. The use of multiple callbacks or chaining asynchronous operations can make the codebase harder to maintain and debug.
- **Error Handling**: Properly handling errors in asynchronous operations can be challenging. Errors occurring in different stages of an asynchronous operation may need to be handled differently, and propagating errors through the asynchronous chain requires careful consideration.
- **Debugging Complexity**: Debugging asynchronous code can be more challenging than synchronous code. Tracking the flow of execution, understanding the sequence of asynchronous operations, and pinpointing the source of errors can require additional effort and expertise.

Despite these challenges, the benefits of asynchronous programming outweigh the difficulties. By leveraging asynchronous programming techniques effectively, developers can create more responsive and performant applications.

In the next sections, we will explore various techniques and tools available in Flutter to facilitate asynchronous programming, including futures, awaits, and async functions, to harness the benefits while addressing the challenges of asynchronous programming.

Futures

In Flutter, a Future represents a value or an error that will be available at some point in the future. It is used to handle asynchronous operations and represents the result of an asynchronous computation. Futures are an essential part of asynchronous programming in Flutter and are widely used to handle operations like network requests, file I/O, and database queries.

A Future can have two possible states: uncompleted or completed. When a Future is uncompleted, it means that the operation it represents is still in progress. Once the operation is complete, the Future becomes completed and holds the result or error of the operation.

Futures can be used to perform tasks asynchronously without blocking the main thread, ensuring a smooth user experience. By using Futures, you can initiate an operation and continue executing other tasks while waiting for the result. Once the operation is completed, you can handle the result or error using callbacks or other asynchronous constructs.

To create a Future in Flutter, you can use the Future class and its various factory methods. For example, you can use the Future.delayed method to create a Future that completes after a specified duration, or you can use the Future.value method to create a completed Future with a specific value.

When working with Futures, you can use various methods and operators to transform and combine them, such as then, catchError, whenComplete, and await. These methods allow you to chain asynchronous operations, handle errors, and perform cleanup tasks once the Future completes.

By using Futures effectively, you can write asynchronous code that is more readable, maintainable, and efficient. Futures enable you to handle asynchronous operations in a structured manner, making it easier to manage complex control flows and handle errors gracefully.

Creating a future

In Flutter, we can create a future using the Future class. The Future class is generic, meaning that it can hold a value of any type. Here's an example of how to create a future that returns an integer value:

```
Future<int> calculateSquare(int n) {
  return Future.delayed(const Duration(seconds: 1), () => n * n);
}
```

Note: If you are unsure of the return data type you can make the return data as dynamic by not declaring it.

```
Future calculateSquare(int n) {
      return Future.delayed(Duration(seconds: 1), () => n * n);
  }
```

In the preceding example, we have created a function called **`calculateSquare`** that takes an integer value and returns a future that will calculate the square of the input value after one second delay.

Handling a future

Once we have created a future, we need to handle its results. We can use the **`then()`** method of the future to handle its result. Here's an example:

```
calculateSquare(2).then((result) {
   print(result);
});
```

In the preceding example, we have called the **calculateSquare** function with an input value of 2. We then used the **then()** method to print the result once it becomes available. The **then()** method takes a function as an argument that will be called once the future is completed.

Handling future errors

When working with asynchronous operations in Flutter, it's crucial to handle errors that may occur during the execution of Futures. In this blog post, we will dive into two approaches for handling Future errors: using the **.catchError** method and employing the try-catch block. We will walk through examples to demonstrate their usage and provide practical insights into error handling in Flutter.

Handling future errors with .catchError method

The **.catchError** method allows us to specify a callback function that will be invoked when an error occurs in the Future. Here's an example that demonstrates its usage:

```
Future<int> fetchData() {
  return Future.error('Error occurred while fetching data!');
}

void handleFutureError() {
  fetchData()
    .then((result) {
      // Handle successful result
    })
    .catchError((error) {
      // Handle the error
      print('Error: $error');
    });
}
```

In the above code snippet, the **.catchError** method is chained to the Future using the cascade notation (..). It allows us to define a callback function that will be called if an error occurs during the execution of the Future. Inside the callback, we can handle the error by logging it or taking appropriate action.

Handling future by using FutureBuilder

In Flutter, we can use the **FutureBuilder** widget to display the result of a future. The **FutureBuilder** widget takes a future and a builder function as arguments. The builder function is called once the future completes, and it returns the widget that should be displayed based on the future's result. Here's an example:

```
Future<int> calculateSquare(int n) {
  return Future.delayed(Duration(seconds: 1), () => n * n);
}

class MyApp extends StatelessWidget {
  @override
  Widget build(BuildContext context) {
    return MaterialApp(
      title: 'Flutter Demo',
      home: Scaffold(
        body: Center(
          child: FutureBuilder<int>(
            future: calculateSquare(2),
            builder: (context, snapshot) {
              if (snapshot.hasData) {
                return Text('Square of 2 is ${snapshot.data}');
              } else if (snapshot.hasError) {
                return Text('Error: ${snapshot.error}');
              }
              return CircularProgressIndicator();
            },
          ),
        ),
      ),
    );
  }
}
```

In the preceding example, we have used the **`calculateSquare(int n)`** function as the **`FutureBuilder`** widget's Future object and a builder function that builds a widget tree based on the value of the completed Future. If the snapshot contains data, it will show a text with the data. If it is being read, it will show a **`CircularProgressIndicator`** else show an error if the result contains an error.

Main difference between `FutureBuilder` and Firebase Firestore listener is that `FutureBuilder` is used to handle asynchronous operations that may complete in the future, while Firebase Firestore listener is used to listen to changes in the Firestore database in real-time.

Await

Asynchronous programming is a crucial aspect of building responsive and efficient Flutter applications. When dealing with asynchronous operations, it's essential to wait for the completion of certain tasks before proceeding to the next steps. The await keyword plays a significant role in achieving this synchronization.

In Flutter, the await keyword is used within an async function to pause the execution of the function until a Future is completed. It allows you to work with asynchronous code in a more sequential and readable manner, as if it were synchronous.

By using await, you can wait for the result of a Future and then proceed with the execution of the function once the Future completes. This eliminates the need for cumbersome callback functions or complex event-driven architectures, making your code more structured and easier to follow.

Here's a brief overview of how await works in Flutter:

1. **Marking a Function as async**:

   To use await, you need to mark the surrounding function with the async keyword. This signals that the function contains asynchronous code and will make use of await to handle Future objects.

2. **Pausing Execution with await**:

   When encountering the await keyword, the function pauses its execution and allows other code to run. It waits for the completion of the Future object that follows the await keyword.

3. **Resuming Execution**:

   Once the Future completes, the function resumes execution from where it left off after the await statement. It can then process the result of the Future and continue with the remaining code.

4. **Error Handling with try-catch**:
   You can use a try-catch block to handle any exceptions that might occur during the execution of the awaited Future. This allows you to gracefully handle errors and perform appropriate actions as needed.

The await keyword is a powerful tool in Flutter that simplifies asynchronous programming and enables you to write code that is more readable and maintainable. It helps ensure that tasks are executed in the desired order and provides a more synchronous-like programming experience.

Here is an example of how to use await in Flutter:

```
Future<String> getWelcomeMessage() async {
  await Future.delayed(Duration(seconds: 3));
  return "Welcome to my app!";
}

void printMessage() async {
  String message = await getWelcomeMessage();
  print(message);
}
```

In the preceding code, we have defined a function **`getWelcomeMessage()`** that returns a Future that resolves to a welcome message after 3 seconds of delay. In the **`printMessage()`** function, we use await to wait for the completion of the **`getWelcomeMessage()`** Future and then print the message.

Async

Asynchronous programming is an essential aspect of building responsive and performant Flutter applications. In many cases, we need to perform time-consuming operations such as fetching data from an API or reading from a file, without blocking the main UI thread. Flutter provides the async keyword to facilitate asynchronous programming and make it easier to handle such tasks.

In Flutter, the async keyword is used to mark a function as asynchronous. An asynchronous function can perform operations concurrently, allowing other code to execute while it waits for the completion of certain tasks. By using async, you can write code that appears to execute synchronously, even though it is actually performing asynchronous operations.

Using Async

The async keyword is used to indicate that a function is asynchronous. An asynchronous function returns a Future object, which represents the result of the operation. The await keyword is used to wait for the result of a Future object, without blocking the main thread.

Let's take a look at some common examples of using async and await in Flutter:

- **Network requests**

  Fetching data from an API is a common task in mobile app development, and it often requires performing network requests asynchronously. Here is an example of using async and await to fetch data from a REST API:

```
Future<List<Post>> fetchPosts() async {
  final response = await http.get(Uri.parse('https://
jsonplaceholder.typicode.com/posts'));
  if (response.statusCode == 200) {
    final List<dynamic> json = jsonDecode(response.body);
    return json.map((e) => Post.fromJson(e)).toList();
  } else {
    throw Exception('Failed to load posts');
  }
}
```

  In this example, the **fetchPosts** function returns a **Future<List<Post>>** object, which represents the result of the API call. The await keyword is used to wait for the **http.get** function to return a response before continuing. If the response status code is 200, the function converts the JSON response into a list of Post objects using the **fromJson** constructor.

- **File operations**

  Working with files is another common task in mobile app development, and it often requires asynchronously performing file operations. Here is an example of using async and await to read the contents of a file:

```
Future<String> readFile(String path) async {
  try {
    final file = File(path);
    return await file.readAsString();
  } catch (e) {
    return 'Error reading file: $e';
  }
}
```

In this example, the `readFile` function returns a `Future<String> object`, which represents the contents of the file. The await keyword is used to wait for the `file.readAsString` function to return the contents of the file before continuing.

Conclusion

In conclusion, Futures, await, and async are crucial concepts in asynchronous programming in Flutter. By using these tools, developers can create more responsive and efficient applications that handle complex tasks without blocking the user interface. Futures allow developers to work with values that may not be available immediately, while async and await provides a simplified way to write asynchronous code that is easy to read and maintain. In addition, understanding how to use these concepts effectively can help developers create more reliable and scalable applications. With practice and experience, developers can leverage these tools to create high-performance applications that delight users.

In the next chapter, we will delve into the fascinating world of Persistence and Data Modelling in Flutter. We will explore various techniques and best practices for storing and managing data in your Flutter applications.

Task

Continuing from the previous task, complete the following. In case you cannot get through, you can access our GitHub repository (**https://github.com/lahirunc/task_tracker**) and get the solution. Each task has its specific branch.

Moving forward, the instructions may seem complicated. Therefore, the book will be providing you with the entire code snippets, but we encourage you to figure out and use snippets and repositories as the last resort. Try to do some trial and error. If an error is found, try doing a Google search. You'll find many just like you and I have asked help from others in the community.

1. Add Future and Await for all the queries except the listener in our Flutter Task project.

Questions

1. **What is a Future in Flutter?**
    a. A widget that represents a loading state
    b. A function that returns a value sometime in the future
    c. A widget that shows a message to the user
    d. None of the above

2. **How do you wait for a Future to complete in Flutter?**
    a. Use a FutureBuilder widget
    b. Use an Await expression
    c. Use an Async function
    d. Use a StreamBuilder widget
3. **What is an async function in Flutter?**
    a. A function that can run concurrently with other code
    b. A function that must run sequentially with other code
    c. A function that cannot return a value
    d. None of the above
4. **Which keyword is used to mark a function as async in Flutter?**
    a. Async
    b. Future
    c. Await
    d. None of the above
5. **What is the purpose of the await keyword in Flutter?**
    a. To pause execution until a Future completes
    b. To cancel a Future
    c. To force a Future to complete immediately
    d. None of the above

Answers

1. **b**
2. **b**
3. **a**
4. **a**
5. **a**

References

- **https://dart.dev/codelabs/async-await**
- **https://dart.dev/guides/libraries/futures-error-handling**

Chapter 8
Persistence and Data Modeling

Introduction

Flutter persistence and data modeling are crucial topics for building scalable and efficient mobile applications. With Flutter, developers have access to a variety of tools and libraries to manage data storage and manipulation.

In this chapter, we will explore different approaches for data modeling in Flutter and how to persist data using local storage options such as shared preferences. We will also dive into using cloud-based storage solutions such as Firebase Realtime Database and Cloud Firestore. Finally, we will discuss best practices for handling data synchronization between client and server and provide examples of how to implement data caching to optimize app performance. By the end of this chapter, you will have a solid understanding of the different options available for managing data in your Flutter applications.

Structure

In this chapter, we will cover the following topics:

- Data models
- Creating data models with factory methods
- Storing data on to the device

Data models

Creating data models in Flutter is an essential step when it comes to managing and manipulating data in your application. Data models are representations of real-world objects that your application needs to interact with. They define the structure and type of data that is passed around in your application, making it easier to handle and manipulate the data.

To create data models in Flutter, you need to define classes that represent the objects that you want to interact with. For example, if you are building a social media application, you might need to create data models for users, posts, comments, and likes. Each of these models will have their own properties and methods that are specific to their use case.

Here's an example of a simple data model for a user in Flutter:

```
class User {
  String name;
  int age;
  String email;

  User({required this.name, required this.age, required this.email});
}
```

In this example, the User class has three properties: name, age, and email. These properties are defined using the String and int data types. The User class also has a constructor that takes in the values for these properties when a new User object is created.

Once you have created your data models, you can use them to manage and manipulate data in your application. For example, you might create a list of User objects that you can display in a list view or use to filter and sort data.

Creating data models is an important step in building any Flutter application. It helps to ensure that your data is well-organized, easy to manage, and can be easily passed between different components of your application.

Factory methods

In Flutter, a factory method is a static method that returns an instance of a class. Unlike a regular constructor, a factory method can return a cached object or an object of a subclass. Factory methods can also be used to control the object creation process and to provide better encapsulation. The factory keyword is used to define a factory method in Dart.

Creating data models with factory methods

To create a data model with a factory method in Flutter, we first define a class that represents our data model. We then define a factory method that returns an instance of the class. Let's create an example data model for a social media app:

```
class User {
  String name;
  int age;
  String email;

  User({required this.name, required this.age, required this.email});

  factory User.fromJson(Map<String, dynamic> json) {
    return User(
      id: json['name'],
      title: json['age'],
      description: json['email'],
    );
  }

  Map<String, dynamic> toJson() {
    return {
      'name': name,
      'age': age,
      'email': email,
    };
  }
}
```

In the preceding code, we have defined a User class with three properties: name, age, and email. We have also defined a constructor for the class that initializes the properties. The factory User.fromJson method is used to create a User instance from a JSON object. We have also defined a toJson method that converts a User instance to a JSON object.

To use the User data model in our app, we can create a new instance of the class by calling the constructor:

```
final user = User(
  name: 'John',
  age: 25,
```

```
  email: 'john@gmail.com',
);
```

We can also create a User instance from a JSON object by calling the factory method:

```
final json = '{"name": "John", "age": 25, "email": "john@gmail.com"}';
final user = User.fromJson(jsonDecode(json));
```

We have explored the concept of factory methods and how to create data models with factory methods in Flutter. Factory methods are a powerful technique that can be used to control the object creation process and to provide better encapsulation. By using factory methods, we can create data models that are easy to use and maintain, and that provide a well-structured format for interacting with the data.

Storing data on to the device

Flutter provides various options for storing data locally in the device, such as Shared Preferences, SQLite, and Hive. One of the easiest and simplest options is Shared Preferences, which is a key-value pair storage mechanism. We will focus on how to use Shared Preferences to store data in the device in Flutter.

Shared Preferences are used to store small amounts of data that need to be persisted between application launches. This data can be in the form of key-value pairs, where the key is a unique identifier, and the value can be any data type. In Flutter, Shared Preferences are implemented using the **`shared_preferences`** package.

First, we need to add the **`shared_preferences`** package (*Figure 8.1*) to our pubspec.yaml file and run flutter packages to get in the terminal to install it.

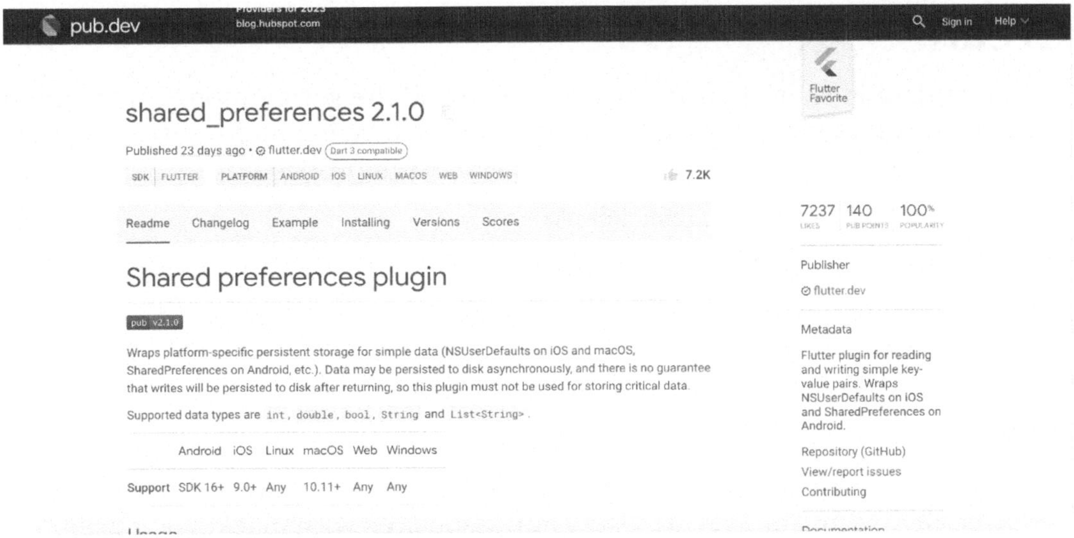

Figure 8.1: *Shared Preference pub.dev page* (***https://pub.dev/packages/shared_preferences***)

To use Shared Preferences, we need to instantiate an instance of SharedPreferences, which can be done as follows:

```
SharedPreferences prefs = await SharedPreferences.getInstance();
```

This will return a shared preference instance that we can use to read and write data.

Creating a shared preference instance can be an expensive operation, especially if you need to retrieve or update data frequently. To avoid this, it is recommended to create a single shared preference instance and reuse it throughout the app. This can be achieved by creating a singleton class that handles the creation of the shared preference instance and provides static methods for accessing and updating the data. This approach ensures that the shared preference instance is created only once and avoids the unnecessary overhead of creating a new instance every time you need to access or update data. We will discuss how to do it in the task outlined in this chapter.

Create

To create data in shared preferences, we can use the set method. This method takes a key-value pair as input, where the key is a string and the value can be either a string, integer, boolean, or double. For example:

```
prefs.setString('name', 'John Doe');
prefs.setInt('age', 30);
prefs.setBool('isLogged', true);
prefs.setDouble('score', 9.5);
```

Read

To read data from shared preferences, we can use the get method. This method takes the key as input and returns the value associated with that key. For example:

```
String name = prefs.getString('name');
int age = prefs.getInt('age');
bool isLogged = prefs.getBool('isLogged');
double score = prefs.getDouble('score');
```

Update

To update data in shared preferences, we can simply call the set method with the same key and a new value. For example:

```
prefs.setInt('age', 31);
```

Delete

To delete data from shared preferences, we can use the remove method. This method takes the key as input and removes the key-value pair associated with that key. For example:

```
prefs.remove('score');
```

Conclusion

Persistence and data modeling are essential concepts in Flutter that help developers create efficient, scalable, and maintainable applications. By properly designing and implementing data models, developers can ensure that their application's data is well-structured and easy to access. Additionally, by leveraging persistence mechanisms such as shared preferences, developers can store data on the device and provide an excellent user experience. Finally, proper CRUD operations on the stored data can help developers manage the data and provide meaningful interactions to the users. It is crucial to have a good understanding of these concepts to build high-quality and reliable Flutter applications.

In the next chapter, we will be discussing important topics such as changing the app name, adding an app icon, versioning the app, building the app and releasing it to the app stores. These topics are crucial for creating a professional and successful app that can compete in the market.

Task

Continuing from the previous task, complete the following. In case you cannot get through you can access our GitHub repository (**https://github.com/lahirunc/task_tracker**) and get the solution. Each task has its specific branch.

Moving forward, the instructions may seem complicated. Therefore, the book will be providing you with the entire code snippets, but we encourage you to figure out and use snippets and repositories as the last resort. Try to do some trial and error. If an error is found, try doing a Google search. You'll find many just like you and I have asked help from others in the community.

This task has two parts. The first part is to add a greeting message with our user's name in our HomeScreen. Every time user visits HomeScreen they will be greeted as shown below (*Figure* 8.2). The second part is the modelling of data received from Firebase Firestore. Let's get coding!

Figure 8.2: *HomeScreen with the greeting*

Part 1

1. Add the text inside the HomeScreen as shown in *Figure* 8.2. Use the following for the edit button.

```
IconButton(
          icon: const Icon(
            Icons.edit,
            size: 20,
          ),
          onPressed: () {},
        )
```

2. Create a folder named utils under the lib folder and inside the utils folder create local_storage.dart file (*Figure* 8.3).

Figure 8.3: *lib folder*

3. Create an instance of shared_preference called onInit().

```
import 'package:shared_preferences/shared_preferences.dart';

class LocalStorage {
  static late final SharedPreferences prefs;

  static Future<void> init() async {
  prefs = await SharedPreferences.getInstance();
  }
}
```

4. Open main.dart file and inside the main() function call the onInit() function.

```
Future<void> main() async {
        // this is needed for firebase to be initialized
        WidgetsFlutterBinding.ensureInitialized();

        // init firebase
        await Firebase.initializeApp(
          options: DefaultFirebaseOptions.currentPlatform,
        );

        // init shared preferences
        await LocalStorage.init();

        runApp(const MyApp());
      }
```

5. Inside LocalStorage class and add another function named saveString with parameters String key and String value. Inside the saveString function add the code to save a String value.

```
static Future<void> saveString(String key, String value) async {
                await prefs.setString(key, value);
}
```

6. Next, write a function named readString with a parameter String key to read the saved String.

```
static String? readString(String key) {
    return prefs.getString(key);
  }
```

7. Create the following **AlertDialog** (*Figure* 8.4) inside the IconButton onPressed method. You'll need a Column widget and use this code snippet inside the Column to resize it.

```
mainAxisSize: MainAxisSize.min,
```

Figure 8.4: *AlertDialog*

8. In *Figure* 8.4, when ElevatedButton is pressed it should validate the content inside the TextFormField the same way we did in **CreateTaskScreen**. You can define **GlobalKey** and **TextEditingController** inside the showDialog builder function.

9. After validating the form, we are going to save the content in TextFormField to our local storage. This value will be the name that will be shown in the greeting. To do that write the following code inside the onPressed method.

```
onPressed: () async {
                 if (formKey.currentState!.validate()) {
// name is the key
      await LocalStorage.saveString('name',
textEditingController.text).then((value) {
      // after saving this will close the dialog
```

```
            Navigator.pop(context);
            });
        }
    },
```

10. Next, we need to show the saved value as our greeting. Also, we want to show a default value if the value is null. Define a String name between the build function and return Scaffold. Then call LocalStorage.readString() function and pass in the key.

```
// If name is null, ?? will assign 'User' to String name
      String name = LocalStorage.readString('name') ?? 'User';
```

Note: The ?? operator is called the null-aware coalescing operator. It is used to provide a default value when a variable is null. If the variable is not null, the expression evaluates to the variable's value, otherwise it evaluates to the default value provided.

11. Finally, to display the value, just append the text as follows.

```
Text(
    'Hello $name',
     style: const TextStyle(
          fontSize: 18,
          fontWeight: FontWeight.bold,
     ),
),
```

Part 2

Let's create a data model for our Firebase Firestore data. This will help us to handle our data easily.

1. Create a folder called "models" inside the lib directory.
2. Inside the "models" folder create a task_model.dart file and create a class TaskModel
3. Add the following to the model:
    a. String? id
    b. String? task
    c. bool? Status
    d. fromJson()
    e. toJson()

4. Inside HomeScreen, before initState() create a new List that accepts TaskModel called taskList.

```
List<TaskModel> taskList = [];
```

5. Next, inside the Firebase Firestore listener, add the following

```
firestore.collection("tasks").snapshots().listen((QuerySnapshot event) {
      // clearing data in the list
      taskList.clear();

      for (var task in event.docs) {
        // converting the object into map
        Map<String, dynamic> taskMap = task.data() as Map<String,
                                                       dynamic>;

        // adding task id
        taskMap['id'] = task.id;

        // set state to refresh the UI when the data is added
                                                   setState(() {
          // adding TaskModel into task list
          taskList.add(TaskModel.fromJson(taskMap));
        });
      }
```

6. Next, wrap a Listview.builder widget around the TaskTile (*Figure* 8.5) and give itemCount as taskList.length. Adding Listview.builder will cause an error. Try to debug and solve it on your own. In case you got stuck answer is on the GitHub Repository.

Figure 8.5: *TaskTile*

7. Access data inside the list by taskList[index].task! and taskList[index].status

8. Update the status of the task when the user taps on the checkbox.

Tip: Write the Firebase Firestore update query inside the onChanged function of the checkbox.

9. Next, add two IconButtons to Edit and Delete each task. Refer to *Figure* 8.6. A Row widget can be used as follows.

```
Row(
    // mainAxisSize.min force Row to take the min. space
              mainAxisSize: MainAxisSize.min,
              children: [
                Checkbox(
                  value: taskList[index].status,
                  onChanged: (value) {},
                ),
              ],
            ),
```

Figure 8.6: *TaskTile with edit and delete buttons*

10. Write the code to delete the task when the Delete button is tapped.
11. Create an edit_task_screen.dart file inside the screen folder and create a form the same as the **`CreateTaskScreen`**. Change **`Create Task`** to **`Edit Task`** and the button text from **`Create`** to **`Update`**.
12. Pass the task as TaskModel to EditTaskScreen into a variable called TaskData.
13. Create an initState() function and write the following code. This will assign a default value to the TextFormField.

```
textEditingController.text = widget.taskData.task!;
```

14. Finally, write the update query inside the **`Update`** button. The value of the status should not be changed.

Congratulations! You have successfully created a fully working Flutter app with CRUD functionalities.

Multiple Choice Questions

1. **What is the purpose of data modeling in Flutter?**
    a. To create UI components
    b. To structure and organize data in a logical way
    c. To handle user input in forms
    d. None of the above.

2. **What is persistence in Flutter?**
    a. It is the process of saving and retrieving data
    b. It is the process of rendering UI components
    c. It is the process of connecting to a database
    d. It is the process of testing an app
3. **Which method in Flutter is used to store data on the device?**
    a. `SharedPreferences.saveData()`
    b. `DataStorage.save()`
    c. `PersistentData.save()`
    d. `SharedPreferences.save()`
4. **What is the purpose of the await keyword in Flutter?**
    a. To indicate that a method is asynchronous
    b. To pause the execution of a method until a future completes
    c. To retrieve data from a database
    d. None of the above
5. **Which method in Flutter is used to retrieve data from shared preferences?**
    a. `SharedPreferences.getData()`
    b. `SharedPreferences.getString()`
    c. `SharedPreferences.get()`
    d. `SharedPreferences.retrieve()`

Answers

1. b
2. a
3. d
4. b
5. b

References

- **https://docs.flutter.dev/development/data-and-backend/json**
- **https://pub.dev/packages/shared_preferences**

Chapter 9
Deploying

Introduction

Deploying an app is the final step in the app development process, and it's a crucial one. The way you deploy your app can impact its success in the market, and it's important to get it right. Flutter is a popular cross-platform mobile app development framework, and deploying Flutter apps is easy, thanks to its built-in toolset.

In this book chapter, we'll dive into the deployment process for Flutter apps. We'll explore everything from changing the app name to adding an app icon, versioning, building, and releasing. By the end of this chapter, you'll have a solid understanding of how to deploy your Flutter app and get it in the hands of your users.

First, we'll start by discussing how to change the app name. A memorable and unique app name can go a long way in creating a strong brand identity. We'll explore how to update the app name both in the code and in the app stores.

Next, we'll discuss adding an app icon. A well-designed app icon can make your app stand out on users' devices and help create a recognizable brand. We'll show you how to create an app icon and add it to your Flutter app.

Versioning is an important aspect of app deployment. It enables you to keep track of changes in your app and communicate those changes to your users. We'll discuss how to version your Flutter app and what you need to keep in mind.

The final step in deploying your Flutter app is building and releasing it. We'll explore how to build an APK or an IPA file for Android and iOS respectively, and how to release your app on the app stores.

Deploying a Flutter app can seem daunting, but with the right tools and knowledge, it can be a smooth process. This book chapter will provide you with everything you need to know to deploy your Flutter app successfully. So, let's get started!

Structure

In this chapter, we will cover the following topics:

- Changing the app name
- Adding app icon
- Versioning
- Building and Releasing

Changing the app name

When building a mobile application in Flutter, one of the important aspects is to give it an appropriate and unique name. However, there might be situations where you want to change the app name after developing the app.

The first step to change the app name is to open the project's pubspec.yaml file, which contains information about the project's dependencies and assets. In the pubspec.yaml file, you will find a field called **`name:`**. This field is where you can change the name of your Flutter app. Simply update the name field with your desired app name, save the file, and the changes will take effect.

```
name: new_app_name
```

After changing the app name, it is recommended to run the Flutter packages get command in the terminal to update the dependencies of the project.

The next step is to update the app name in the AndroidManifest.xml file. This file contains important information about your app, such as the app name, version, and activities. To change the app name, navigate to the **android/app/src/main/AndroidManifest.xml** file, and find the application element. In this element, you will find the android:label attribute. Change the value of the **`android:label`** attribute to the new app name.

```
<application
      android:name="io.flutter.app.FlutterApplication"
      android:label="New App Name"
      android:icon="@mipmap/ic_launcher">
```

Next, we need to change the app name in the Info.plist file for iOS. To do this, navigate to the ios/Runner/Info.plist file, and find the **CFBundleName** key. Change the value of the CFBundleName key to the new app name.

```
<key>CFBundleName</key>
      <string>New App Name</string>
```

After updating both the AndroidManifest.xml and Info.plist files, save the files and rebuild the app. Once the app is rebuilt, you will see the new app name reflected on your device.

In conclusion, changing the app name in Flutter is a simple process that involves updating the name field in the pubspec.yaml file, updating the **android:label** attribute in the AndroidManifest.xml file, and changing the value of the CFBundleName key in the Info.plist file for iOS. With these steps, you can easily update the app name in your Flutter app.

Adding an app icon

Adding an app icon is an essential part of creating a mobile app, as it helps to identify your app visually. In Flutter, adding an app icon is a straightforward process.

Adding simple app icon

Adding an app icon is a crucial step in giving your Flutter application a unique and visually appealing identity.

1. In the project directory, navigate to the '/android/app/src/main/res' folder. Here you will see a folder named 'mipmap'. This folder contains the different sizes of the app icon that we need to provide.

2. Create an image that you want to use as an app icon. Make sure the image size is at least 192×192 pixels, and it's in the PNG format.

3. Rename the image as 'ic_launcher.png' and copy it to the '/android/app/src/main/res/mipmap' folder. You need to replace the existing 'ic_launcher.png' file with your new image.

4. Now navigate to the '/ios/Runner/Assets.xcassets/AppIcon.appiconset' folder. Here you will see different sizes of the app icon that we need to provide for the iOS platform.

5. Create an image that you want to use as an app icon. Make sure the image size is at least 1024x1024 pixels, and it's in the PNG format.

6. Rename the image as 'AppIcon.png' and copy it to the '/ios/Runner/Assets.xcassets/AppIcon.appiconset' folder. You need to replace the existing 'AppIcon.png' file with your new image.

7. Finally, run the app on an Android or iOS device to see the updated app icon.

Adding an adaptive app icon

Flutter also allows for more complex app icons, such as animated app icons or adaptive app icons. To create an adaptive app icon, you can use the Flutter 'flutter_launcher_icons' package, which allows you to generate app icons for different platforms and devices.

To use the flutter_launcher_icons package (*Figure* 9.1), first, add it to your project by adding the following lines to your pubspec.yaml file.

```
dev_dependencies:
  flutter_launcher_icons: "^0.13.1"

// To customize the app icon, you can modify the configuration settings in
// your pubspec.yaml file.
flutter_launcher_icons:
  android: "launcher_icon"
  ios: true
  image_path: "assets/icon/icon.png"
  min_sdk_android: 21 # android min sdk min:16, default 21
  web:
    generate: true
    image_path: "path/to/image.png"
  windows:
    generate: true
    image_path: "path/to/image.png"
    icon_size: 48 # min:48, max:256, default: 48
  macos:
    generate: true
    image_path: "path/to/image.png"
```

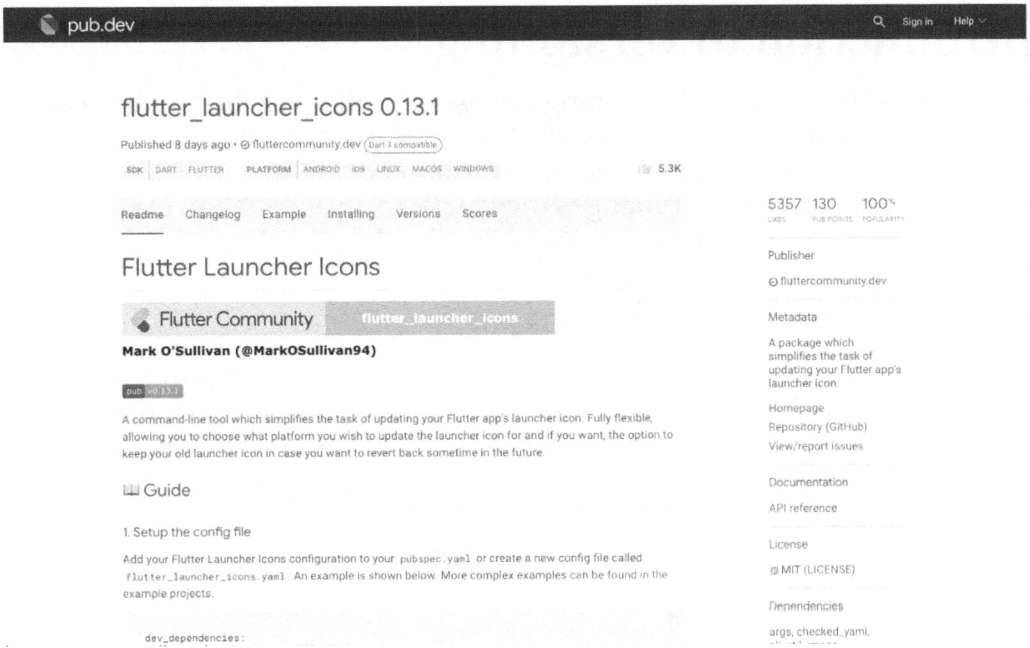

Figure 9.1: *flutter_launcher_icons package in pub.dev* (***https://pub.dev/packages/flutter_launcher_icons***)

Once you have added the package, you can generate your app icon by running the following command in your terminal:

```
flutter pub run flutter_launcher_icons:main
```

Note: You have to run above command every time you change the *flutter_launcher_icons* configurations.

This will generate the app icon in the appropriate sizes and formats for both Android and iOS. By default, the icon will be placed in the android/app/src/main/res directory for Android and the ios/Runner/Assets.xcassets/AppIcon.appiconset directory for iOS.

In conclusion, adding an app icon in Flutter is a quick and easy process. By following the steps outlined above, you can easily replace the default app icon with your own custom image. It's a small but important step in creating a visually appealing and recognizable mobile app.

Versioning

Versioning is an essential part of software development as it helps developers keep track of different releases of an application. In Flutter, versioning is crucial for both the development process and the release process.

Introduction to versioning

Versioning is the process of assigning unique identifiers to different releases of an application. These identifiers usually take the form of numbers or strings, and they indicate which version of the application is being used. Versioning helps developers keep track of the changes they make to an application over time, and it makes it easier to communicate which version of the application is being used.

Importance of versioning

Versioning is important because it allows developers to keep track of the changes they make to an application. By assigning unique identifiers to each release, developers can easily reference previous versions of the application and compare them to the current version. This makes it easier to identify bugs, track down issues, and ensure that the application is functioning as intended.

Implementing versioning in a Flutter application

In Flutter, versioning can be implemented using the pubspec.yaml file. This file contains metadata about the application, including the version number. The version number is a string that can be updated to reflect the current version of the application.

To implement versioning in a Flutter application, follow these steps:

1. Open the pubspec.yaml file in your Flutter project.
2. Locate the version line and update the version number to reflect the current version of the application.
3. Save the pubspec.yaml file.

For example, the version line in the pubspec.yaml file might look like this:

```
version: 1.0.0+1
```

In this example, the version number is "1.0.0+1". The first three numbers (1.0.0) represent the version of the application, while the last number (1) represents the build number. The build number is incremented each time a new build of the application is created.

Versioning is an important part of software development, and it's essential for Flutter applications as well. By implementing versioning in your Flutter project, you can keep track of changes, identify bugs, and ensure that your application is functioning as intended. The pubspec.yaml file is an easy way to implement versioning in your Flutter application, and it's recommended that you update the version number regularly as you make changes to your application.

Building and releasing

Building a release version of a Flutter app is a crucial step in the app development process. It involves creating an optimized build of the app that can be uploaded to the app store or shared with others.

Building

Android

When you are ready to release your Flutter app on the Google Play Store, you need to build a release version of your app.

Step 1: Set up the app for release mode

Before building the release version of the app, we need to make sure that the app is set up for release mode. Open the terminal or command prompt and navigate to the root directory of the Flutter app. Then run the following command:

```
flutter build apk --release
```

This command generates a release build of the app in the form of an APK file.

Step 2: Create a keystore file

To sign the release build of the app, we need to create a keystore file. A keystore file is a secure container that holds the app's signing key. Run the following command to create a keystore file:

```
keytool -genkey -v -keystore myapp.keystore -alias myapp -keyalg RSA
-keysize 2048 -validity 10000
```

Replace myapp with the name of your app.

Step 3: Configure the app to use the keystore file

In the android/app/build.gradle file, add the following lines of code to configure the app to use the keystore file:

```
android {
    ...
    signingConfigs {
        release {
            keyAlias 'myapp'
```

```
                keyPassword 'password'
                storeFile file('path/to/myapp.keystore')
                storePassword 'password'
            }
        }
        ...
}
```

Replace myapp with the name of your app and password with your keystore password.

Step 4: Build the release version of the app

Now that the app is set up for release mode and the keystore file is configured, we can build the release version of the app. Run the following command:

```
flutter build apk -release
```

This command generates a release build of the app in the form of an APK file that is signed with the keystore file.

Step 5: Upload the app to the Play Store

The final step is to upload the release build of the app to the Play Store. Each app store has its own process for uploading apps, so be sure to follow the instructions provided by the Play Store.

Login to your Google Play Console, select **`All Apps`** and click on **`Create app`** (*Figure* 9.2).

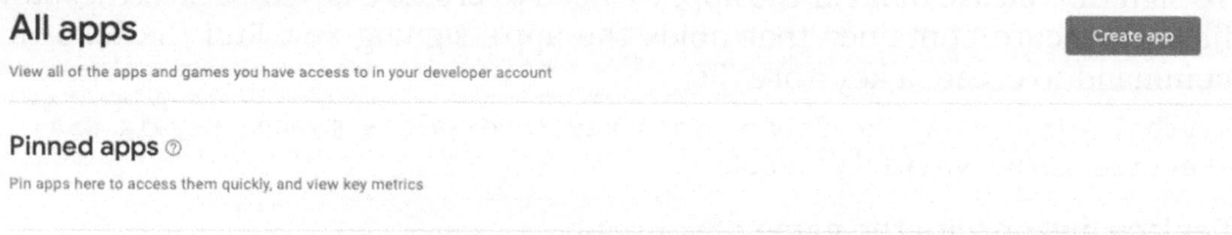

Figure 9.2: *Google Play Console – All Apps*

You are greeted with below *Figure* 9.3. Update the details, accept the declarations and click on the **`Create App`** button

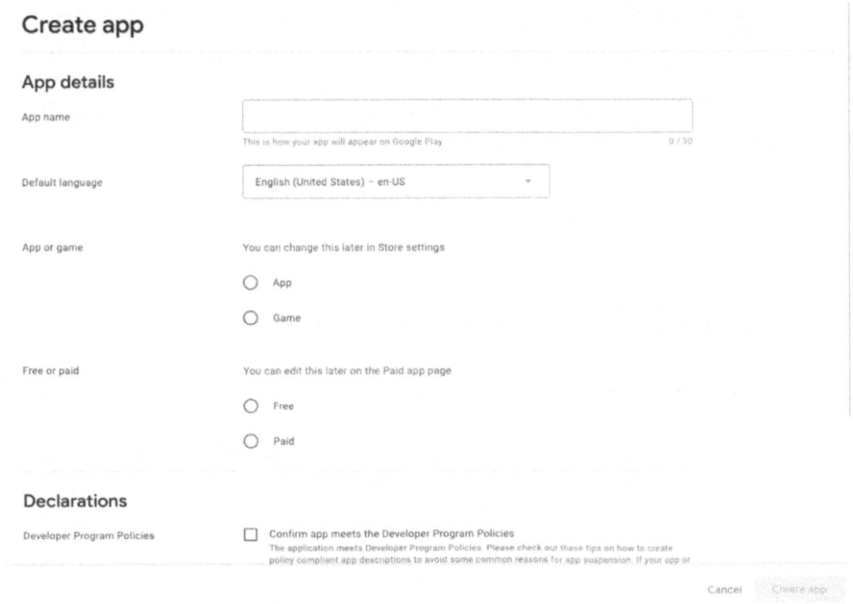

Figure 9.3: *Google Play Console – Creating App*

A set of tasks will be given as shown in *Figure* 9.4. Complete them to release your app to Google Play Store. Once you have completed all the app details and reviewed your app, you can publish your app to the Play Store by clicking on the **`Publish`** button.

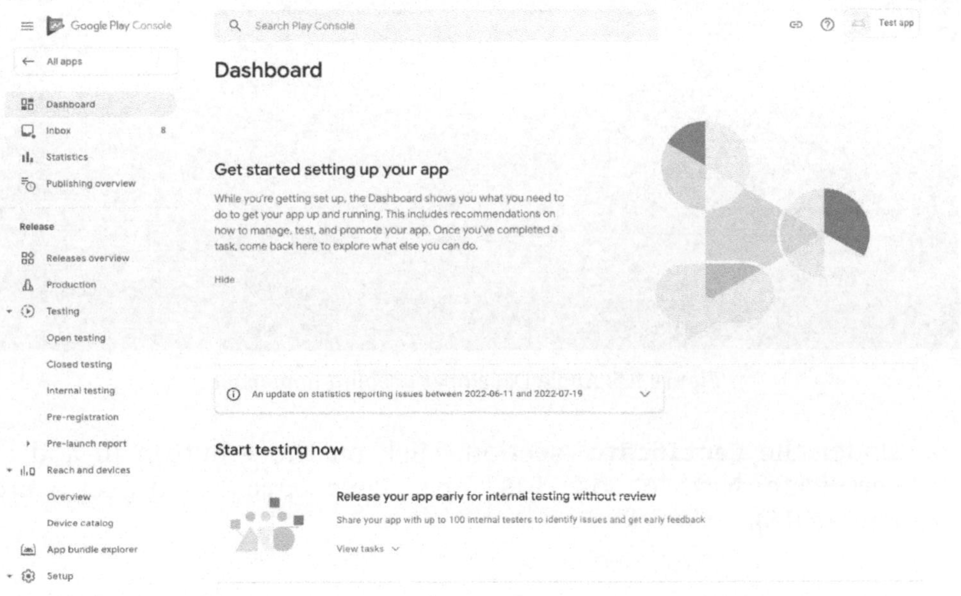

Figure 9.4: *Google Play Console – App Dashboard*

Once you have published your app, it will go through a review process by the Google Play team. This can take anywhere from a few hours to a few days.

Once your app has been reviewed and approved, it will be available for download on the Play Store. Congratulations, you have successfully uploaded your Flutter app to the Play Store!

iOS

Having a Mac device is a must to build your iOS release.

Step 1: Set up your app for release

Before you can build your app for release, you need to make sure that your app is set up correctly. This includes making sure that you have a valid distribution certificate and provisioning profile. You can create these in your Apple Developer account.

a. To add a certificate, log in to your Apple Developer account and click on the Certificates under Certificates, IDs & Profiles (*Figure* 9.5).

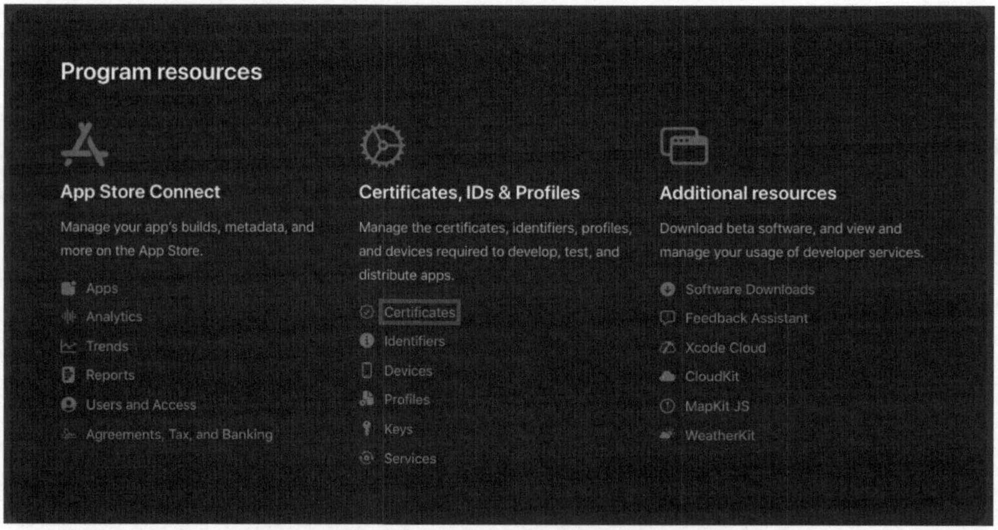

***Figure* 9.5**: *Apple Developer account homepage*

b. Under the **`Certificate`**" section, click on the **+** button to add a new certificate. Next, choose **`iOS App Development`** and click **`Continue`** (*Figure* 9.6).

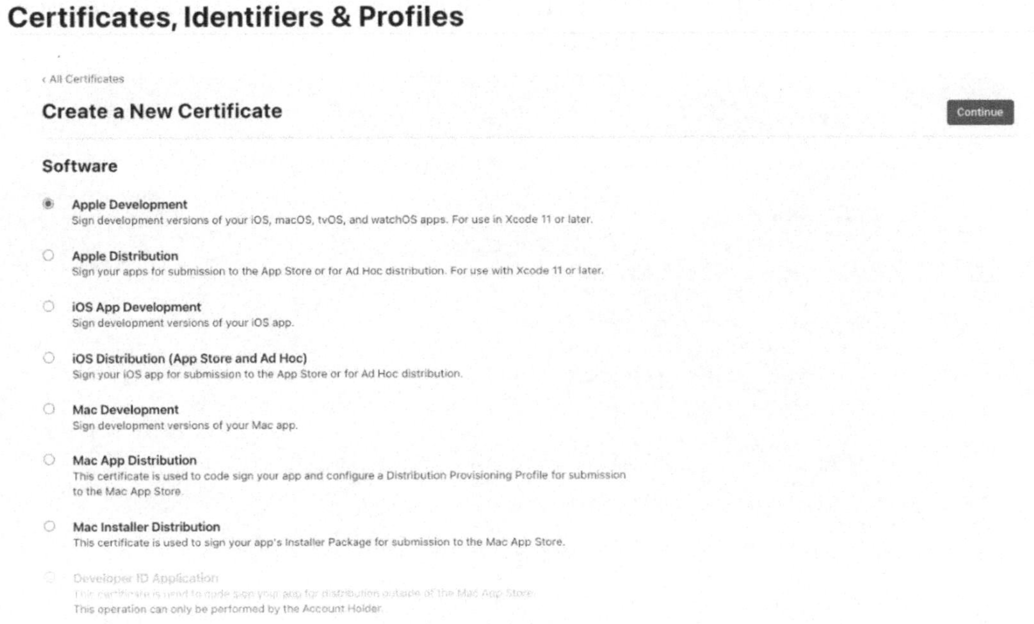

***Figure 9.6**: Creating a New Certificate*

c. Follow the instructions on the screen shown in *Figure* 9.7 on generating a Certificate Signing Request (CSR) using Keychain Access on your Mac. Then Upload the CSR to your Apple Developer account and click **`Continue`**.

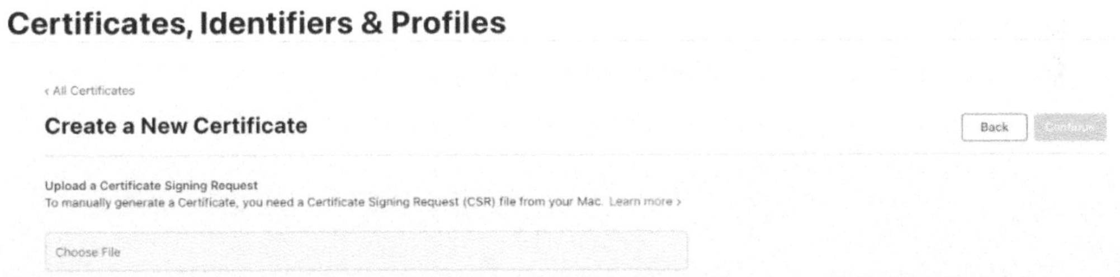

***Figure 9.7**: Uploading the Certificate Signing Request*

d. Download the distribution certificate and add it to your Keychain Access on your Mac. Next, add the app as an identifier. To do that open the

Flutter app using XCode (Open the iOS folder using XCode) and locate the Bundle Identifier (*Figure* 9.8).

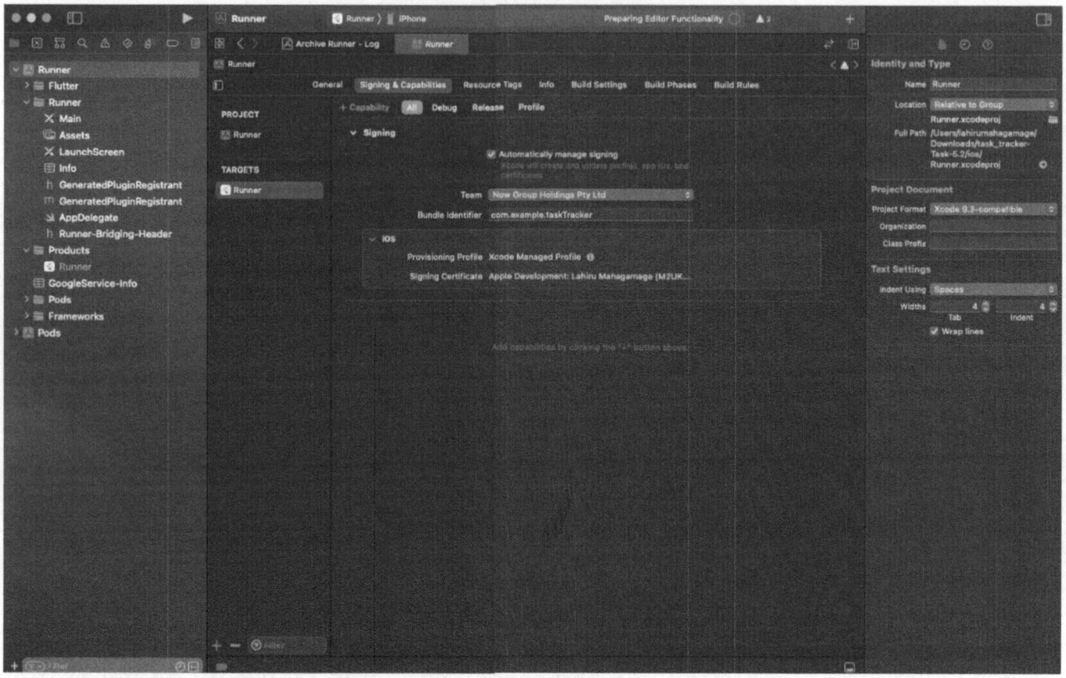

Figure 9.8: *Flutter Project on Xcode*

e. Under **`Certificates, Identifiers & Profiles`**, select **`Identifiers`** and click on the **+** button to register a new identifier (*Figure* 9.9).

Figure 9.9: *Identifiers tab in Certificates, Identifiers & Profiles*

f. Select **`App IDs`** and click **`Continue`** (*Figure* 9.10).

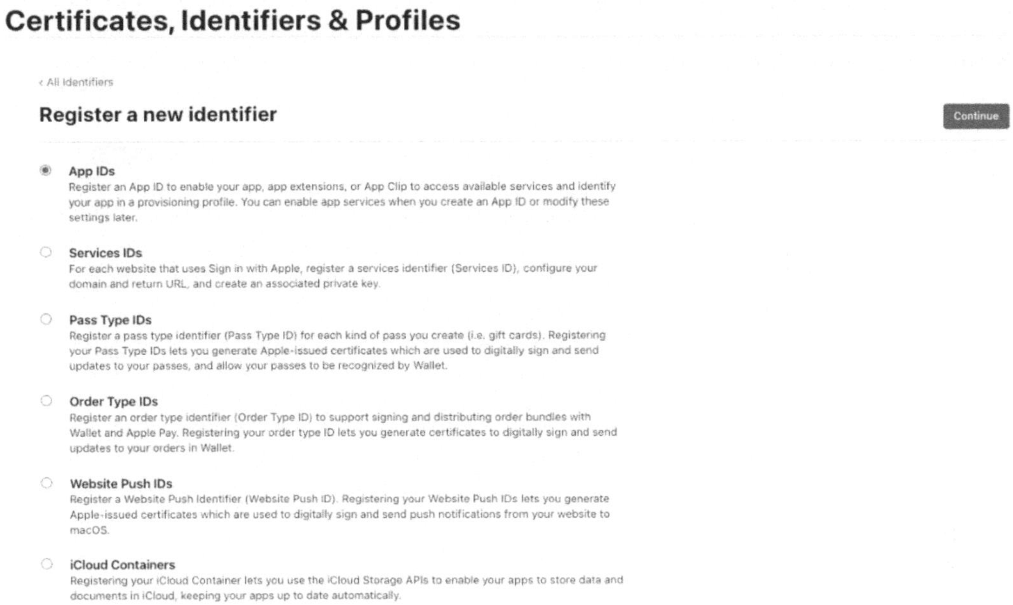

Figure 9.10: *Register a new Identifier*

g. Select the type as **`App`** and click **`Continue`** (*Figure* 9.11).

Figure 9.11: *Select a Type*

h. Update the Description and Bundle Id which we found in *Figure* 9.10. Following shown is the **`Register an App ID`** page (*Figure* 9.12). In addition to the above, you can enable/disable all the Capabilities and App Services you need for your app here.

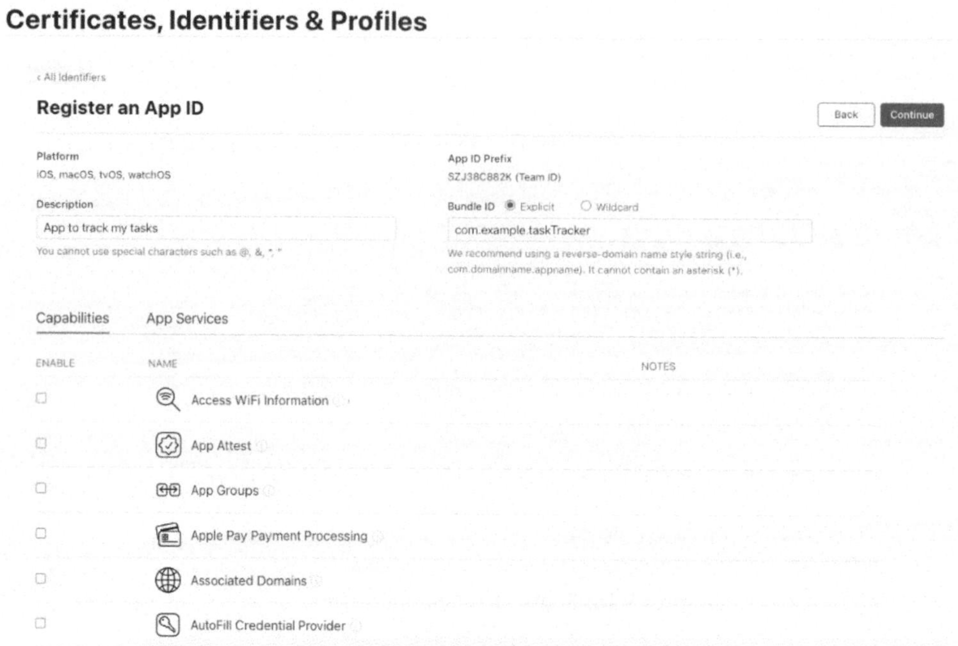

Figure 9.12: *Register an App ID*

i. Finally, click on **`Continue`** and follow the prompts shown on the screen.

Step 2: Building the app

Before uploading a Flutter app into the AppStore, you need to build a release. Open Xcode and select **`Product`** from the menu and click on **`Archive`** to build (*Figure* 9.13).

f. Select **App IDs** and click **Continue** (*Figure* 9.10).

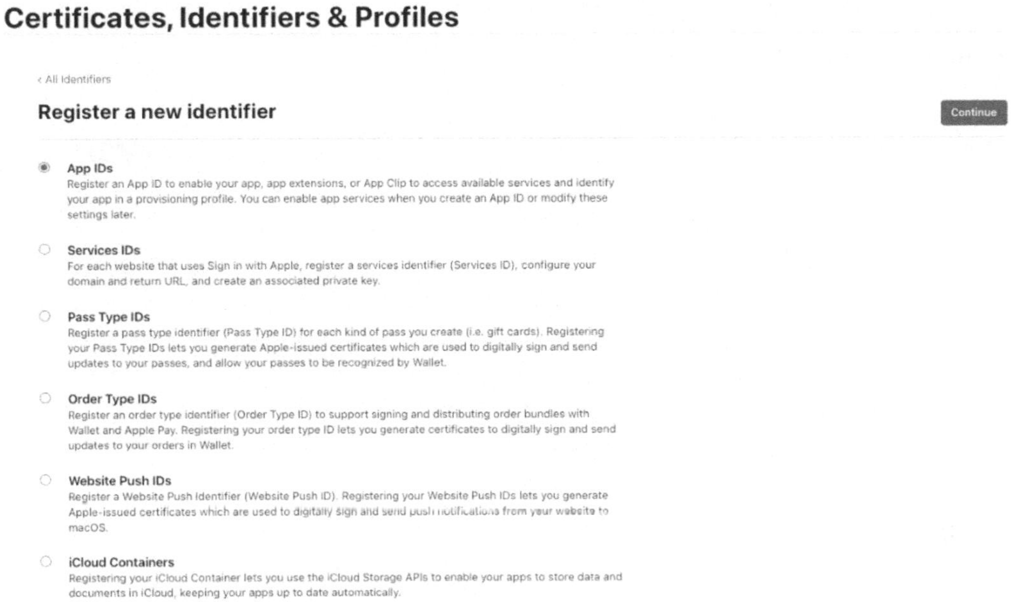

***Figure* 9.10:** *Register a new Identifier*

g. Select the type as **App** and click **Continue** (*Figure* 9.11).

***Figure* 9.11:** *Select a Type*

h. Update the Description and Bundle Id which we found in *Figure* 9.10. Following shown is the **Register an App ID** page (*Figure* 9.12). In addition to the above, you can enable/disable all the Capabilities and App Services you need for your app here.

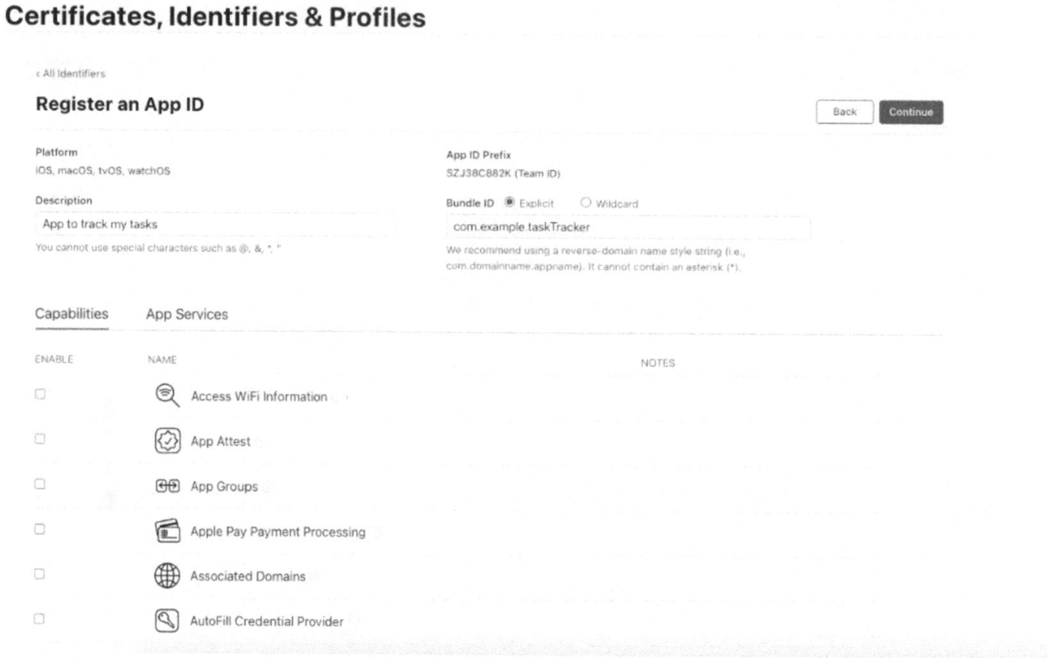

Figure 9.12: *Register an App ID*

i. Finally, click on **`Continue`** and follow the prompts shown on the screen.

Step 2: Building the app

Before uploading a Flutter app into the AppStore, you need to build a release. Open Xcode and select **`Product`** from the menu and click on **`Archive`** to build (*Figure* 9.13).

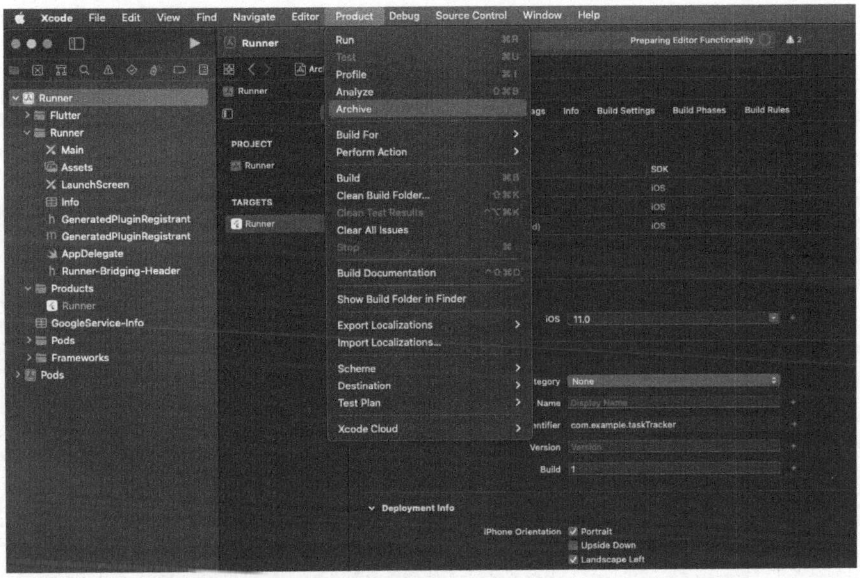

Figure 9.13: *Flutter Project on Xcode – Product Menu*

Tip: You can use *flutter build ipa* to create a release and use Transporter app from AppStore for Mac.

Step 3: Uploading the app to AppStore

Once the build is complete, select the **`Distribute App`** option and click **`Next`** (*Figure 9.14*).

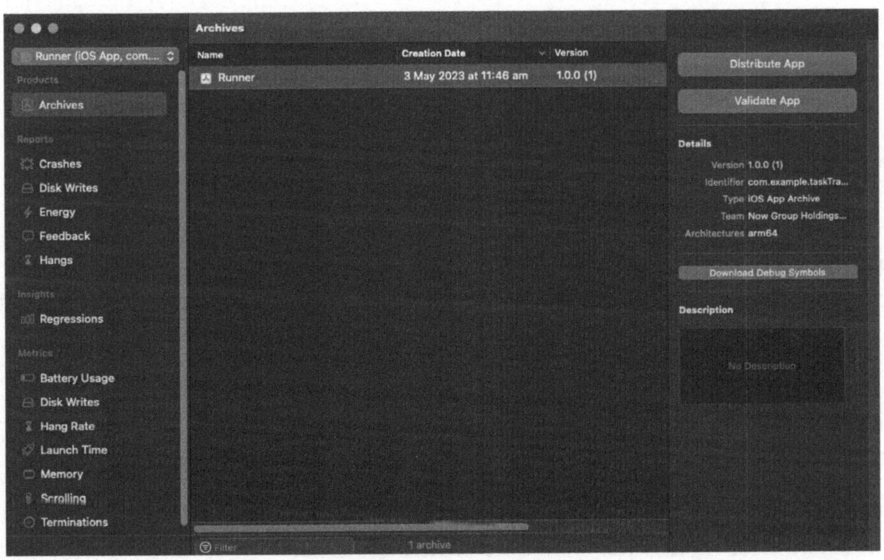

Figure 9.14: *XCode Archives*

Choose **App Store Connect** as the distribution method and click **Next** (*Figure 9.15*).

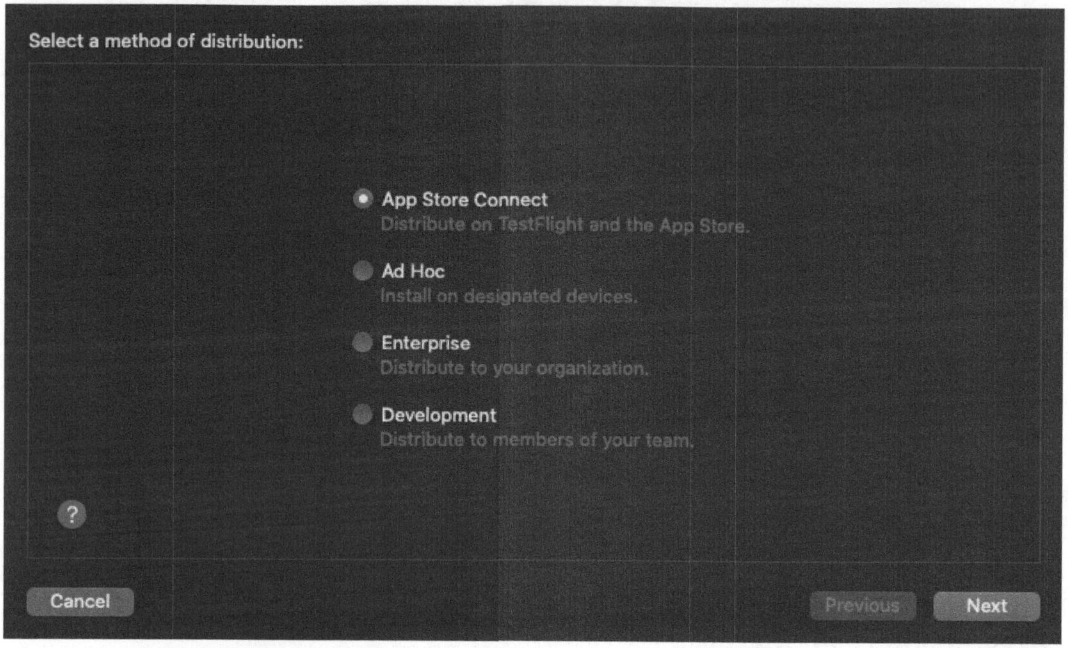

Figure 9.15: XCode – *Select a method of distribution Window*

Select **Upload** and click on **Next**. Finally, follow the prompts on the screen and upload your Flutter app.

Once your app has been reviewed and approved, it will be available for download on the App Store Congratulations, you have successfully uploaded your Flutter app to the App Store!

Conclusion

In conclusion, deploying a Flutter app involves several steps such as changing the app name, adding an app icon, versioning, building, and releasing. Each step is crucial for a successful app deployment and requires attention to detail.

Changing the app name is a simple process that can be done by updating the app name in the project's configuration files. Adding an app icon is also relatively easy, and the flutter_launcher_icons package can be used to generate app icons for both Android and iOS.

Versioning is an essential aspect of app development and deployment, and it involves assigning a unique version number to each release of the app. This helps users identify and update to the latest version of the app.

Building and releasing the app involves several steps, such as creating a release build, signing the app, and submitting it to the respective app stores. The flutter build command can be used to create a release build, and the flutter build apk command can be used to create an Android package file for distribution.

In this book, we have covered several topics related to Flutter, such as widgets, state management, Firebase, persistence, and deploying the app. We hope that you have enjoyed your learning journey and are now equipped with the knowledge and skills to develop awesome Flutter apps.

Now it's time to go out and create some amazing apps. Happy coding!

Task

Continuing from the previous task, complete the following. In case you cannot get through you can access our GitHub repository (**https://github.com/lahirunc/task_tracker**) and get the solution. Each task has its specific branch.

Using what you learned from this chapter, try to upload your app to the AppStore or Play Store.

Multiple Choice Questions

1. **What is the purpose of changing the app name in Flutter?**
   a. To make the app name more interesting
   b. To make the app name more memorable
   c. To avoid name conflicts in the app store
   d. None of the above

2. **Which package can be used to add app icons in a Flutter app?**
   a. flutter_icons
   b. flutter_launcher_icons
   c. flutter_app_icons
   d. flutter_icon_pack

3. **What is versioning in Flutter?**
   a. The process of adding features to an app
   b. The process of updating an app's UI
   c. The process of assigning a unique number to each app release
   d. None of the above

4. **What is the purpose of building and releasing in Flutter?**
   a. To make the app faster
   b. To fix bugs in the app
   c. To deploy the app to the app store
   d. None of the above

5. **How can you build a Flutter app for release?**
   a. Run the command 'flutter build app'
   b. Run the command 'flutter run --release'
   c. Run the command 'flutter build apk'
   d. Both b and c

Answers

1. **c**
2. **b**
3. **c**
4. **c**
5. **d**

References

- **https://docs.flutter.dev/deployment/android**
- **https://pub.dev/packages/flutter_launcher_icons**

Note: *Depending on your system, you may need to restart any open terminal or command prompt windows for the changes to take effect. Additionally, keep in mind that if you move the Flutter SDK to a different location, you will need to update the PATH accordingly.*